Y0-BTD-946

Land Reform

in Relation to Social Development

EGYPT

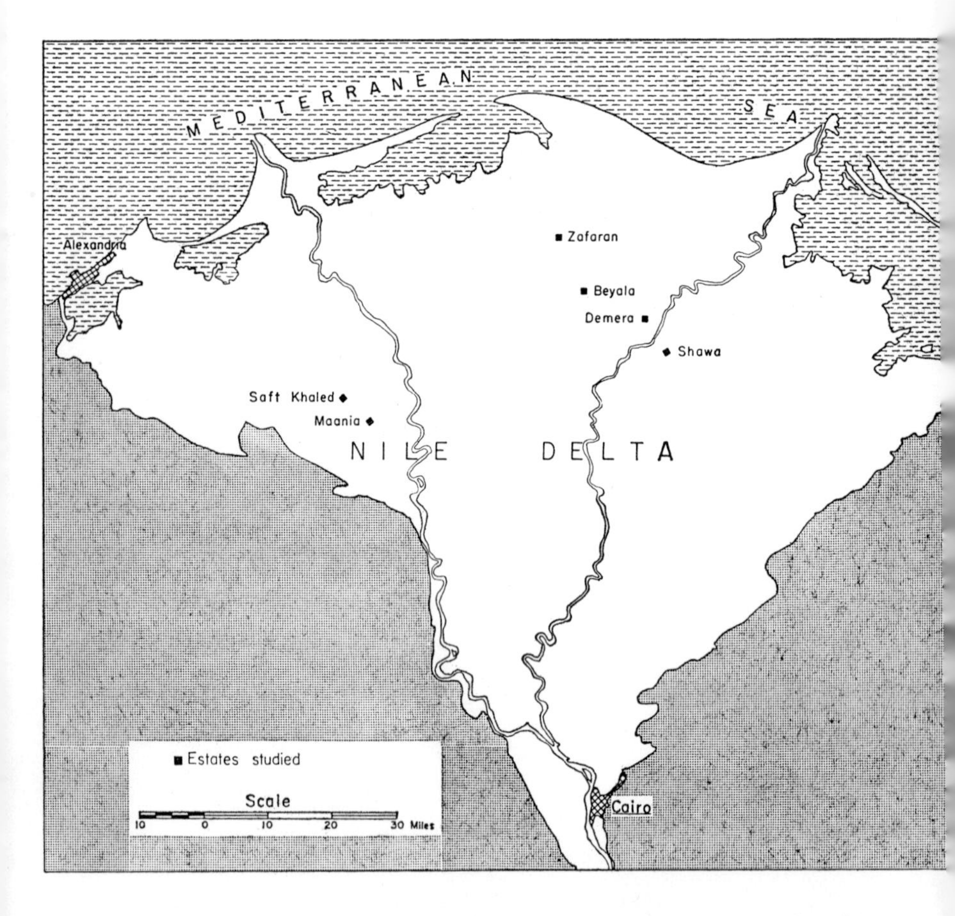

Map of the Nile Delta showing location of the estates analyzed in this study: the land-reform estates, Demera, Zafaran, and Maania; and the Wakf estates, Shawa, Beyala, and Saft Khaled, not subject to expropriation and redistribution, which were selected as controls.

Land Reform in Relation to Social Development EGYPT

SAAD M. GADALLA

UNIVERSITY OF MISSOURI STUDIES VOLUME XXXIX

University of Missouri Press • Columbia

Library of Congress Catalog
Card Number 62-14208

Printed and bound in the United States of America

TO MY FATHER

in gratitude for his invaluable love, understanding, and patience

Foreword

It is a pleasure to recommend this volume to the reading public, for it represents no ordinary treatise on land reform. Saad Gadalla, a native son of Egypt, has provided a reliable and excellent picture of agriculture and rural life in his native country. Financed by a fellowship from the Population Council of New York, he returned to Egypt after extended study in rural sociology and spent a full year collecting the information upon which this book is based, doing all of the field work himself. Returning to the University of Missouri, where he had already spent two years of study, he tabulated and analyzed his material and produced a 500-page manuscript that served as a dissertation for the Ph.D. degree which he received in 1960. This volume represents a condensation of the findings of the dissertation, enriched by Dr. Gadalla's life-long familiarity with rural life in Egypt.

Over a long period of human history, land reform measures have been widely advocated and often used as a device to equalize more fully the land resources among those who were wont to till the soil. The present volume constitutes a significant contribution to the literature of this problem. It tells the story of an agrarian people who undertook land-reform measures to provide better living conditions for those who farm, and to remedy the inequities of the tenure system which contributed to instability, insecurity, and unrest. In times past, many such attempts at land redistribution have been made by various peoples. Probably such measures will continue to be attempted if population continues to increase and good land resources become relatively scarce. Dr. Gadalla's contribution provides a good summary and analysis of one of the most recent attempts. Doubtless it will be consulted for many years to come.

Charles E. Lively

Acknowledgements

THE author appreciates very much the advice and assistance given him at various stages of the study by a number of experts and scholars. At the University of Missouri, Professors Charles E. Lively and Robert L. McNamara of the Department of Rural Sociology have been able advisors and critics at all stages of the work. Professor Cecil L. Gregory assisted greatly in the statistical analysis. Other members of the Department of Rural Sociology offered helpful suggestions for the revision of the manuscript. Mrs. Marjorie S. Roberts, Instructor in Education, proofread the manuscript.

In Egypt, Mr. Sayed Morei, former Minister of State for Agrarian Reform, greatly facilitated the field work. The officials of the Higher Committee for Agrarian Reform rendered diligent service toward the success of the investigation. The Egyptian farmers welcomed the author generously into their homes and provided the information upon which this study is based.

To all of these, the author wishes to express his sincere thanks while absolving them of the responsibility for errors of fact or judgment. The author is particularly grateful for the four-year leave of absence granted by the Egyptian Higher Committee for Agrarian Reform and for the two-year fellowship grant from the Population Council which supported this study. Neither the Higher Committee nor the Population Council, however, is to be understood as approving, by virtue of these grants, any statement made or view expressed in this study.

S.M.G.

Contents

Contents

Tables

APPENDIX

UNITS OF MEASUREMENTS

One Feddan = 1.038 acres

One Hectare = 2.471 acres

One Egyptian Pound (£E): Before 1933 £E 1.00 was equivalent to $5.00 in United States currency; between 1933 and 1949, £E 1.00 was worth $4.12; since 1949 and until the present time, £E 1.00 has been worth $2.87.

CHAPTER I

The Problem and Perspective

LAND in Egypt is valued not for itself alone; its possession is a form of security, a symbol of prestige, and a source of power. For many years a conflict of interest between the "haves" and the "have nots" dominated the social, economic, and political scenes. The reactionary policies of the landlords created an atmosphere of antagonism between the elite minority and the majority, landless farm people. This antagonistic feeling grew until several open revolts broke out in the countryside: land hunger became a crucial problem demanding urgent consideration. On September 9, 1952, the revolutionary government of Egypt attempted to satisfy the wild hunger of the landless by enacting the Agrarian Reform Law to improve the living conditions of those who work the land, and to remedy the maladies of the tenure system which contributed to instability, insecurity, and unrest.

This is a study of land reform in relation to the social development of the farm population in Egypt. The data presented were obtained between September, 1956, and August, 1957. The author is aware of the short period which elapsed between the enactment of the Agrarian Reform Law and the time of his field studies, and his justification for the choice of this ambitious subject can be only that it is an important one. This study attempts to give a systematic treatment of the subject or at least some kind of ordered perspective.

CONCEPTUALIZATION OF THE PROBLEM

Land reform is a very ancient idea which has gradually taken different forms. The first reforms were simple programs for dividing the land according to obvious needs. In ancient China, for example, the land was redivided every few centuries so that periodically the people were set on a fresh footing of equality. In the eastern Mediterranean area, the land was redivided among the families every decade or so.[1]

In modern times this elementary idea about land reform has been enlarged to include concern for raising the social status and improving the economic conditions of farm people. John Stuart Mill, for example, formed the Land Tenure Reform Association in 1870, in order to give the greatest encouragement to production. As he stated, "It has been thought right that individuals should have an exclusive property in land, so that they may have the most possible to gain by making the land as productive as they can."[2] The efforts of Mill inspired the enactment of England's land-reform acts, such as the Landlord and Tenant Act, which was followed by the First Agricultural Holdings Act in 1875 and the Tenants Compensation Act in 1890.

In France, Sismondi and Saint-Simon developed similar land-reform ideas. They condemned the system of capitalistic individualism and favored government supervision. Sismondi viewed with alarm the concentration of wealth in the hands of a few, and called for widespread peasant proprietorship to assure happiness and virtue.[3]

On the other side of the Atlantic, the enactment of the Homestead Act of 1862 stemmed from the doctrine that "the man who tills the land ought to own it," and was based on the proposition that true democracy can be achieved only by making ownership of land the backbone of the agrarian and social structure.[4]

Another land-reform issue was raised by Henry George in the United States. He attributed poverty to land speculation and the subsequent concentration of ownership in fewer and fewer hands. He wanted to eliminate monopolies in land tenure by taxing away land rent increments.[5]

Karl Marx advocated the abolition of landlord classes, since, in his opinion, the accumulation of wealth at one pole was, at the same time at the opposite pole the accumulation of misery, agony of toil, slavery, ignorance, brutality, and mental degradation.[6]

In the present century, Pigou stated that "any transference of income from a relatively rich man to a relatively poor man of similar temperament, since it enables more intense wants to be satisfied at the expense of less intense wants, must increase the aggregate sum of satisfaction."[7] Salter tried to indicate that complete freedom of land acquisition and disposal resulted in land overcapitalization, land parcellation, and land monopoly. He stated:

> The mistake we have made has been rather to assume that the system would work automatically—that, once land has been put into private ownership, all of the potential benefits of such ownership would immediately accrue to our society, and, further, that the system would perpetuate itself.[8]

In recent years, land reform has received widespread and serious attention. The General Assembly of the United Nations, the Economic and Social Council, and the Trusteeship Council have frequently discussed the subject and have indicated the need for land reforms and for changes in the agrarian structure of many underdeveloped countries. The Economic and Social Council, at its Thirteenth Session on September 7, 1951, adopted Resolution 370 (XIII), which recommended "that governments institute appropriate land reforms in the interest of landless farmers and those with small and medium-sized holdings."[9] The Council further recommended that the specialized agencies give high priority to the land-reform problem in their technical assistance programs, focus attention on the urgent need for land reform in many areas, and place particular emphasis on assisting governments which wish to adopt land-reform measures. The Council also made provision for the regular review of the progress achieved by governments in land reform. The first report in this respect indicates that extensive and basic measures of agrarian reform have been undertaken in more than sixty countries and territories with a total population of 1,300,000,000 and with agricultural areas amounting to a total of two billion hectares (1 hectare equals 2.471 acres).[10]

Despite the recent overwhelming interest in land reform, the study of the subject tends to remain a fragmented, embryonic specialty rather than a concise, distinctive area of mutually relevant research and thinking. This condition may be attributed to the fact that land reform is an interdisciplinary subject rather than a subject in its own right. It is an academic no-man's land, either a part-time concern, or a specialty without specialists. Economists, sociologists, historians, politicians, and many others discuss the subject and investigate the problem, each using a different approach within a different framework of reference. As a result, the accumulation of literature in the field is confusing on several issues. For example, there appear to be conflicts between the demand for greater social equality and the need for increasing efficiency in agriculture, and between these two objectives and the demographic factor which must be placed in its right perspective. There also appears to be a conflict about the political objectives of the issue. While some people believe that the object of land reform is to defeat Communism, others assert that land reform is Communism.[11]

In fact, there is a difference of opinion as to what land reform really means. Traditionally, the term has been used to mean redistribution of property in land for the benefit of small farmers and agricultural workers. In their replies to the United Nations' questionnaire on progress in land reform, however, many governments included data not only on land redistribution but on a wide range of measures for increasing agricultural production, regulating land use, and improving conditions of tenancy.[12] At the Conference On World Land Tenure Problems at Madison, Wisconsin, Fitzgerald defined land reform as "the changes in agriculture economic institutions which improve the economic, social and political status of the individual occupier of land, and in so doing, contribute to general economic development."[13] Parsons defined the term as "the aggregate of programs for resolving tenure problems."[14]

The object of using such broad definitions is to widen the scope of land reform in order to emphasize that reforms should not only be confined to the redistribution of land, but should also include measures for helping the farmers and increasing the productivity of agriculture. As a result, the definition of land reform is now somewhat confused. Warriner believes that the redistribution of land is far more difficult and controversial than the other measures and cannot be put on a level with other institutional improvements: redistribution of land means a major social and political change, while the other measures lead to improvements in agricultural production and in the economic position of the farmers without a change in their social position.[15]

This point of view was also expressed by the Lebanese Minister, George Hakim:

> As generally used in international discussions, the term "land reform" has come to refer to a wide gamut of prob-

> lems of a legal, social and economic character. This large conception does not give sufficient emphasis to the basic issue of the land tenure system . . . at the heart of the problem of land reform in under-developed countries is the question of who owns the land. This fundamental question has been confused and over-shadowed by the attention paid to other factors such as settlement of legal title to land, agricultural indebtedness, and land taxation, which, though undoubtedly related to the main problem, are not more than manifestation of this, the basic malady of the agrarian structure. . . .[16]

By contrast is Willard L. Thorp's point of view. He stated:

> Nothing can be called land reform which does not have as its basic and primary concern the improved welfare of the man who works the land. The economic and social institutions surrounding his life on the farm must be improved to bring him a higher standard of living and increased psychological satisfaction. There are many who think of land reform primarily as redistribution of the land—as the breaking up of large holdings into small ones. This may be a part of a land reform program but certainly only one part—and not the most important one at that.[17]

Clarence J. McCormick also expressed a similar opinion. He said:

> I hesitate to use the phrase "land reform" . . . the Soviets and their satellites have given that name an unfortunate meaning—a meaning that begins with confiscation and division of large holdings and ends in collectivization. . . . Such misue of the term land reform is bad enough, but what may be even worse in the long run is the notion that land reform means only changing the owners of the land.[18]

The Egyptian government, in undertaking land-reform measures, did not confine its policy to the redistribution of land. Therefore, it is essential for the purpose of this study to use the term "land reform" to mean all organized governmental actions covered by the Egyptian Agrarian Reform Law of 1952. These actions can be summarized under five provisions:[19]

1. Limitation on ownership of agricultural land and expropriation of certain land for distribution among small farmers.
2. Establishment of agricultural co-operative organizations for the farmers who acquired the requisitioned land.
3. Limitations on dividing agricultural land.
4. Regulation of the landlord-tenant relationship.
5. Provisions in regard to the rights of agricultural laborers.

STATEMENT OF THE PROBLEM

The problem of land reform in relation to the social development of the farm population in Egypt can be viewed according to the nature of changes effected. The most obvious change is in the tenure status of the various classes of farm people, resulting from land-reform measures which eliminated the landlord class by expropriation, and raised the status of landless workers and tenants to land-owners. Expropriation measures affected 1,789 landlords each with holdings over two hundred feddans (1 feddan equals 1.038 acres). Land redistribution measures benefited 200,000 farm families comprised of over one million individuals.

The second change is in the general pattern of land distribution, resulting from the land-reform provisions which broke down large estates into a number of smaller farms. The official figure for land liable to expropriation is 656,736 feddans. Redistribution of this land in holdings of from two to five feddans means the creation of about 180,000 new small farm units.

A third change is in the distribution of income between large land-holders and actual cultivators, resulting from the land-reform provisions which reduced rents and fixed annual installments on re-distributed land at a low rate. The difference between the previous annual rents and the reduced rents is a transfer of income to tenants estimated at £E 40,000,000.

A fourth change is in farming practices and operations, resulting from the establishment of obligatory agricultural co-operative organizations for land-reform owners. These co-operatives control crop rotation, undertake marketing of products, and provide the members with farm supplies, machinery, and loans.

A fifth change is in the conditions of tenancy, resulting from land-reform provisions intended to increase security of tenure, regulate landlord-tenant relationships, and eliminate rent jobbers.

A sixth change is in the inheritance practices, resulting from land-reform provisions enacted to prevent undue subdivision and fragmentation of agricultural land.

This brief analysis of the problem on the basis of the changes effected may facilitate understanding of the complexity of the issues involved. Egyptian land-reform provisions introduced changes in man's relation to man in the use and disposition of land. This relation is defined not only by formal and legally enforceable agreements, but also by customary agreements and traditional practices, even more compelling forces. Any change resulting from these provisions may have established, therefore, the basis for new standards in tenure and social relations.

Redistribution of land which changes landless workers and tenant-cultivators to landowners may do more than satisfy the peasant's hunger for land. It may give him the opportunity to move up the social ladder and to free himself from social and economic dependence on landlords. The peasant who acquires ownership of the land may have a new interest in increasing the output from his farm, since anything more he can produce is his alone and does not have to be shared with landlords. He may also gain a feeling of security that greatly changes his attitudes toward his government and his role as a citizen.

The transfer of agricultural income from large landholders to small cultivators may also have considerable effect on the social level of the farmer and his family and on the rural community as a whole. It may increase the purchasing power of the peasant and help him to satisfy his basic needs for food, clothing, and shelter. He may achieve an economic position which enables him and his family to buy better food, better housing, better education, better medical treatment, and better recreation.

The obligatory co-operative organizations established for land-reform owners may free them from hopeless indebtedness and charges for excessive interest rates. It has always been a basic principle of co-operation, however, that membership should be voluntary. The question may be raised as to whether a co-operative organization which requires that all concerned must join can prove as fully co-operative in fact as in name.

Other land-reform provisions may also have had a considerable social effect on the farm population. Regulation of the landlord-tenant relationship affected far more people that the spectacular distribution of land. Cash rents, which were paid on 72 per cent of the cultivated area, have been limited to seven times the land tax and crop-sharing rents to half the produce after all expenses have been deducted. Leases, which must be in writing, and binding for not fewer than three years, are granted only to those who will farm the land personally.

Provisions intended to improve agricultural labor affect a large class of farm people who have no rights in the land. The social and economic conditions of these laborers depend to a very large extent on the level of living of the farmers by whom they are employed permanently or temporarily.

Provisions against fragmentation of holdings are intended to maintain compact, working farm-units which allow rational farming. These provisions, if they are to succeed, must overcome the sacred inheritance laws of Islam, which have been respected and accepted unquestioningly for centuries by rural people.

PURPOSE OF THE STUDY

It is the purpose of this study: (1) to describe the essential features of Egypt's land-reform program; (2) to analyze the effects of land-reform measures on the social level of the farm population in Egypt during the period from 1952 to 1956; (3) to predict the trend of the social changes which have taken place in rural Egypt as a result of land reform; and (4) to recommend further measures for social development of the farm population.

IMPORTANCE OF THE STUDY

The holding and use of land is of the greatest importance for every social system. In a country like Egypt, where 70 per cent of the total population are rural people, the tenure system determines not only the basic economic laws of the nation, but the social laws as well: it is the framework not only for agricultural production but also for the social system. It can contribute considerably to satisfactory social conditions for the farmer and his family, or conversely, can become a detriment to their social status. In either case, the tenure system affects the level of living of farm people, which is largely dependent on the farmers' net income, and which, in turn, determines the farmers' ability to buy adequate food, obtain suitable housing, and afford necessary medical treatment, education, and recreation. A satisfactory tenure system can be helpful in providing the farmer with an income as stable as feasible under local conditions, at a level which permits him to meet his needs as a human being, and to become a valuable and responsible member of the social system.[20]

In recent years there has been an impressive awareness of the benefits of a satisfactory tenure system. Since the end of World War I, land tenure reforms have been received in a favorable international climate of opinion. Reference to the need for land reforms in many underdeveloped countries have been made at various times in the debates of United Nations' organs concerned with the development of such countries. Special attention and recognition were given to the problem by officials in the United States. President Truman, in a broadcast from San Francisco, said:

> We know that the peoples of Asia have problems of social injustice to solve. They want their farmers to own their land and to enjoy the fruits of their toil. That is one of our great national principles also. We believe in the family-size farm. That is the basis of our agriculture and has strongly influenced our form of government.[21]

Secretary of Agriculture Charles F. Brannan, addressing the annual United States Department of Agriculture Outlook Conference in Washington, D. C., stated:

> American people are greatly disturbed by what is happening in other countries of the world. They realize that a part of the unrest in many countries can be traced to insecure and inequitable land tenure. Under these conditions farm people do not feel that they have a stake in the land, or that they are receiving an equitable share of the produce of the land. This brings us to a greater realization that widespread land ownership, security of tenure, and equitable landlord-tenant arrangements are part of the basic fabric of our democratic institutions.[22]

Senator John Sparkman of Alabama, speaking as the United States delegate at the United Nations, set forth in specific terms the interest of his government in proposals for land tenure reforms. He said: "We believe that the land that a man and his family works and on which they make a living ought to belong to him and to his family."[23]

The revolutionary government of Egypt enacted its Agrarian Reform Law on September 9, 1952, with a view to rebuilding Egyptian society on a new basis. President Nasser expressed clearly the significance of this law to the new land-reform owners during a land distribution ceremony when he said:

> This land does not merely signify ownership but symbolizes your freedom, the freedom of your sons and grandsons. This dear land assigned to you is not only a means of improving materially your conditions but elevating you morally and spiritually, imbuing each individual with a sense of dignity, freedom, and equality.[24]

The Egyptian Higher Committee for Agrarian Reform advocates land reform as an overall movement toward social, economic, political, and national development. In its reply to the United Nations' questionnaires relating to Egyptian agrarian reform measures, the Higher Committee stated:

> The principal aims of the actual Egyptian Reform are farsightedly calculated. It is not only reform in the sense of the present and of changing the standing conditions, but it embraces the future and affects in the long run the national economy of the country. . . . It does not only benefit those who become landowners but it affects the welfare of all those who work in agriculture. . . . Land reform, moreover, stimulates industry through the diversion of investments from land speculation to productive enterprise.[25]

Land reform was the issue on which the Egyptian Revolutionary Council decided to take power openly in order to abolish feudalism, which had its roots in big estates, and to create a new class of secure landowners of small holdings. This contention was clearly stated in one of the reports published by the Press Department of the Higher Committee:

> Land reform means the abolishing of that tyrannic system of feudalism that once governed our rural life, and giving full rights to the farmer who had been for long deprived of both his political and civil rights. . . . All previous trials for reform in our rural society, ruled by feudalism, were useless efforts. But after the enforcement of the new military regime in Egypt, a whole society is awakened. With the execution of the land reform scheme, the farmer, once a nonentity, began to feel secure in a society that gave him the right of ownership and the right to live as a respectable citizen.[26]

In view of these major emphases and the serious attention the subject has received recently, the problem of land reform in its relation to social development of the farm population is of the greatest importance.

Chapter II

The Situation Before Land Reform

Before studying Egypt's land reform in relation to social development of the farm population, it is necessary to examine briefly the situation in Egypt before the enactment of the Agrarian Reform Law. The country's land tenure system and demographic position are of particular interest.

I. Land Tenure System

As defined by Renne "Land tenure is a broad term covering all these relationships established among men which determine their varying rights in the use of land. It deals with the splitting of property rights, for their division among various owners, between owners and occupier, between owner or occupier and creditor, and between private owners and the public."[1]

Land tenure, especially in agrarian societies, exerts a considerable influence on the structure and function of social systems. A system of land tenure should be able to establish and maintain farm units of agriculturally rational size, give a degree of flexibility and security to the cultivator and his investment, and provide incentives and opportunities.[2] It should contribute to efficient use of resources, stability of resource productivity, and equal accessibility to resources among individuals.[3] The degree to which a system can achieve these goals is a measure of its success.

A whole complex of tenure problems centered around Egypt's pattern of land holding and use, and contributed considerably to instability, insecurity, and unrest. These problems included unequal distribution of land ownership, small-size farm units, fragmented holdings, few owner-operated farms, insecure farm tenancy, inadequate credit facilities, a dysfunctional "agricultural ladder," and a rigid interrelation among social, economic, and tenure rankings.

UNEQUAL DISTRIBUTION OF LAND OWNERSHIP

The distribution of land ownership in Egypt was, until 1952, extremely unequal. A review of the figures in Table I indicates that

TABLE I

Distribution of Agricultural Land by Size of Holding, Egypt, 1951

Size of holding (feddans)	OWNERS		AREA	
	(000)	Per cent	(000 feddans)	Per cent
1 and under	2,018.1	72.0	778	13.0
Over 1-5	623.8	22.2	1,344	22.5
Over 5-50	148.4	5.4	1,817	30.2
Over 50-200	9.6	0.3	866	14.5
Over 200	2.1	0.1	1,177	19.8
TOTAL	2,802.0	100.0	5,982	100.0

Source: Statistical Pocket Yearbook, 1952.

94.2 per cent of the total landowners held 35.5 per cent of the land, while only 5.8 per cent of the owners held the remaining 64.5 per cent. At the extreme top, 0.4 per cent of the owners held 34.3 per cent of the land. At the extreme bottom, 72 per cent of the owners held 13 per cent of the land.

The figures indicate further that of the 2,800,000 owners, two million owned one feddan or less, with an average holding of about half a feddan, while 2,115 owned more than two hundred feddans, with an average holding of 550 feddans. Among these owners, 188 held more than a thousand feddans with an average holding of 2,600 feddans.

The distribution of land ownership as shown in the table does not reflect the full extent of inequality of land ownership. There was a large section of the farm population which owned no land. Because of the limited industrial activities, these people were forced to depend on agriculture as their only means of livelihood by renting small areas of land, or by working as laborers on the estates of landlords.

SMALL-SIZE FARM UNITS

The average size of a farm in 1947 was six feddans. Farms under five feddans represented 81 per cent of the total, with an average size of 1.4 feddans. Farms of five to fifty feddans accounted for 18 per cent of the total with an average size of 12.4 feddans. Farms over fifty feddans amounted to only 1 per cent of the total with an average size of 173.4 feddans.[4]

According to the Agrarian Reform Distribution Department, the minimum area necessary to insure economic use of the land is three feddans.[5] In 1947, about 69 per cent of the total number of farms were under three feddans in size. These farms were too small to permit application of new techniques or to allow improvement in methods of cultivation. They were even too small to supply the cultivator and his family with a minimum subsistence, or to provide them with full employment on the land.

FRAGMENTED HOLDINGS

The splitting up of a farmholding into numerous plots scattered over a wide area is a result of the Islam inheritance laws which require the subdivision of land property among heirs. In 1950 about 2,500,000 feddans representing 42.5 per cent of the total arable land were subdivided into two million plots, each cultivated separately.[6]

The drawbacks of fragmentation need no emphasis; waste of time and effort, waste in means of production, and the impossibility of rational cultivation are all obvious effects.

FEW OWNER-OPERATED FARMS

The nation had to depend on owner-operated farms for production of fruits, vegetables, poultry, and dairy products. These crops were usually raised by owner-cultivators as secondary enterprises, alongside the principal crops. The intensification of this type of agriculture was hindered as a result both of the low number of large owner-operated farms, and the widespread practice of tenancy, which required particular tenant crops to be grown as a guarantee of rent payments to landowners.

Prior to land reform, ownership was concentrated in a class of landlords who preferred city life and had little or no interest in agriculture. It was common to find a city lawyer, a physician, a merchant, or an industrialist the owner of a large estate. Being from urban or professional classes, absentee landlords usually leased their land and looked upon their estates as a source of social prestige and political power. Most of their savings were invested in purchasing additional land, and very little was devoted to increasing production or improving the area under cultivation. Few owners of large estates directly cultivated their land; hence few estates were farmed efficiently. In most cases, the estates were left to a manager (Nazer) and were neglected by the owner, or were divided into plots which were leased to small tenants.

INSECURE FARM TENANCY

The Department of Agriculture estimated the rented area in 1949 at 3,611,000 feddans, or 60.7 per cent of the total cultivated area.[7] Unfortunately, no estimate can be made of the proportion of tenants to owners because of the lack of statistics and the overlapping between tenure classes.

Farm tenancy in itself is not an unsatisfactory form of tenure where rents are not excessive and where security of tenure is safeguarded by legislation. Indeed, it may help to transfer the land from inefficient owners to more experienced tenants. Before land reform, farm tenancy in Egypt was characterized by exorbitant rent charges and insecurity of tenure. Rents in most cases were higher than the net farm income. According to the Department of Agriculture, the average net revenue per feddan of owner-operated land was £E 16 in 1946-47, and £E 19 in 1947-48, while the average cash rent per feddan was £E 22 and £E 23, respectively, in the same periods.[8]

Such rents provided the landowners who leased their land with a higher income than that which they could obtain by farming the land themselves. Ghonemy found that in the 16,000 feddan royal estate of Kafr-El-Sheikh in Fuadia province, the average net revenue per feddan owned and operated by the estate was £E 5.02 in 1937 and £E 15.30 in 1949, while the cash rent per feddan leased in the same estate was £E 8.10 and £E 36.00, respectively.[9]

The terms under which the land was leased were dictated by the landowners. Except on large estates, most of the leases were not written, but were, by custom, oral agreements. Leases were usually for one year, sometimes for a one-crop period of from four to six months. The landowner had the right to terminate the lease and to expel the tenant for any reason he considered valid. On the other hand, the tenant had no right to claim compensation for his permanent repairs or unexhausted improvements.

The power of the landowner went further, as it was he who fixed the method of rent payment. When crop prices were low, or were anticipated to be, cash rent was preferred. On the other hand, when crop prices were high, or were anticipated to be, sharecropping was preferred. Under the latter arrangement, the landowner usually took all or most of the cotton, and half or more of the wheat, leaving the maize and alfalfa for the tenant and his livestock.[10]

The tenancy system, under these conditions, was prejudicial to land use and production. First, the tenants who held land under such conditions never felt that they had security and stability, nor indeed did they enjoy it. They tried to get the utmost from the land without replenishing the fertility of the soil, and were, therefore, more like miners than farmers. Secondly, production under this tenancy system was concentrated in tenant crops such as cotton, rice, wheat, and sugar cane. Since other countries raised these crops under extensive farming at much lower costs, they were in a position to compete successfully with Egypt's production of such crops in both world and local markets.

INADEQUATE CREDIT FACILITIES

Because the majority of the farm population did not possess sufficient capital to operate a farm, most farmers supplemented the very little they had by obtaining loans at exorbitant rates of interest. The structure of the credit banking system was not adapted to the needs of the landless and small farmers, but was rather adjusted to meet the credit needs of the owners of large estates and plantations. Consequently, in the absence of banking credit facilities, the credit sources available to the peasant-cultivator to finance small-scale agricultural production were local merchants, landlords, usurers, and well-to-do neighbors.

The widespread conditions of poverty and ignorance among the farm population tempted many cultivators to spend the money they borrowed for non-productive purposes, and they therefore were unable to pay not only the debt itself, but also the accumulated interest. This led to such a continuous increase in land foreclosures that in 1913 the government had to issue a decree stipulating that holdings under five feddans could not be expropriated in repayment of loans.[11] Although this decree protected the small owners, it completely handicapped them from seeking credit through land banks which required security and guarantee for loan payments. It was not until 1931 that the government established the Agricultural Credit Bank to provide small owners with loans for farming expenses. This bank, although successful to some extent in reducing the power of money-lenders and in reducing the interest rates, was incapable of satisfying the demands of tenants because of its complicated loan processes and restrictions.

DYSFUNCTIONAL "AGRICULTURAL LADDER"

Inheritance was the principal way of acquiring land ownership in Egypt before land reform. Land for sale was extremely limited because most land was owned by a few landlords who looked upon their land as a source of social prestige and political power.

There were three possibilities for buying land. One possibility was the newly reclaimed land sold by land reclamation companies and by the Public Domain Bureau in the Egyptian government, but the land reclamation process was very slow and most of the reclaimed land was purchased by big landowners. According to the Public Domain Bureau, the total area sold by the Bureau during the period from 1935 to 1949, was 182,623 feddans. Out of this area, only 3,111 feddans or 1.7 per cent was purchased by small farmers.[12] The second possibility for buying land was at auction sales of mortgaged land when its owners failed to pay their debts to the Agricultural Land Bank. The third possibility arose when small owners were forced sometimes to sell parts of their land in order to meet expenses of occasional obligations such as marriage, pilgrimage, and serious medical treatment.

As a result of this narrow market in land and the increase in farm population over the limited cultivated area, the average prices per feddan rose from £E 119 in 1930 to £E 315 in 1945 and to £E 430 in 1947. Official figures of the Ministry of Agriculture indicate that the average net income per feddan owned and operated in 1947-48 was £E 17.50, and the interest rate was 9 to 10 per cent. The capitalized value of a feddan, therefore, should have been £E 185, and not £E 430 as it actually was.[13]

Most farm people were tenant-cultivators and landless laborers who seldom had the opportunity to acquire land ownership or to progress from lower to higher tenure status. The average tenant was burdened with exorbitant rent and was tied to his landlord by severe terms. The high rent and the debt burden prevented him from accumulating the capital necessary to purchase land. A tenant, in 1947, would have needed £E 2,350 ($9,682) to buy five feddans. Thus he had no other alternative but to stay on the tenancy rung of the agricultural ladder. Even worse was the case of agricultural laborers. Since the average daily wage paid these laborers was ninety-four millims (39 cents) in 1947, the capital required to buy five feddans was equivalent to their wages for 21,850 working days, or sixty years.[14] The agricultural laborer had no choice but to go on working as a laborer.

Agricultural land, being overcapitalized and overvalued, was beyond the economic reach of most people. Except through inheritance, landless farmers had extremely limited opportunities to acquire land and thus advance up the agricultural ladder.

RIGID INTERRELATION AMONG SOCIAL, ECONOMIC, AND TENURE RANKINGS

Social rank in Egypt was closely related to the tenure rights a given individual had in using the land. Owners, who had the right to dispose of their land at will, outranked tenant-cultivators and landless laborers who had fewer rights. As a result the land had a value other than its profit potential: its significance extended far beyond its economic use to influence all aspects of life. Tenure rank or relation to land determined one's status-role, the types of services and payments he was expected to render, and the social patterns of his association and interaction.

Table I of pre-reform land ownership distribution indicates how the size of holdings delineated the various social classes in Egypt. The few landlords who owned two hundred feddans or more formed the upper-upper social class. They were the aristocracy of birth and wealth whose land was inherited through several generations. Generally, they exercised all the power and prestige in the country, dominated the two houses of Parliament, and controlled the lives of those attached to their land. They tended to intermarry, and hence were frequently related to each other by complicated kinship ties. Skilled in ritual behavior and intricate codes of etiquette, the landlords were the social arbiters of the society.

Owners with holdings of from fifty to two hundred feddans formed the lower-upper social class. They were similar in many respects to the upper-upper class but were less influential politically and socially. Owners with holdings of from five to fifty feddans formed the upper-middle social class. They were respected members of the rural community, regarded as persons of importance, and were usually the key leaders. Small owners with holdings of from one to five feddans formed the lower-middle social class. They were eager, hard-working conservatives, and were often considered the backbone of the Egyptian village. The vast majority of landowners held not more than one feddan and formed the upper-lower social class. Though they were much poorer than the classes above them, they were still "respectable." Respectable is what the landless farmers were not. They ranked below all landed groups and formed the lower-lower social class. To this class belonged the tenant-cultivators and landless laborers. Among them, in order of rank, were cash tenants, sharecroppers, permanent laborers, and casual laborers.

Table II, showing pre-reform distribution of gross farm income, indicates how the size of farm operation delineated the various economic classes in Egypt. At the extreme top were operators of more than two hundred feddans. They received 23 per cent of the income and represented only 0.3 per cent of the farmers. At the extreme bottom were operators of not more than one feddan. They received only 4 per cent of the income and represented 37 per cent of the farmers. Between the two extremes of poverty and wealth lay three economic classes. In the first were the operators of from more than one to five feddans, who received 19 per cent of the income and represented 43 per cent of the farmers. In the second were the operators of from more than five to fifty feddans, who received 36 per cent of the income and represented 18 per cent of the farmers. In the third were the operators of from more than fifty to two hundred

TABLE II

Distribution of Gross Farm Income
by Size of Farm, Egypt, 1947

Size of farm (feddans)	FARM OPERATORS		GROSS INCOME	
	Number	Per cent	£E	Per cent
1 and under	373,692	37.36	10,405,855	4.26
Over 1-5	432,428	43.24	46,035,391	18.59
Over 5-50	178,368	17.85	88,117,346	36.30
Over 50-200	12,831	1.28	43,643,819	17.85
Over 200	2,744	0.27	56,228,224	23.00
TOTAL	1,000,063	100.00	244,430,635	100.00

Source: Agricultural and Economic Statistics, Bureau of Agricultural Economics and Statistics, Department of Agriculture, Cairo, Egypt, 1949, p. 39; and National Income from Agriculture, Government Press, Cairo, Egypt, 1948, p. 24.

feddans, who received 18 per cent of the income and represented 1.3 per cent of the farmers.

The delineation of social and economic classes clearly shows the strong interrelation among social, economic, and tenure rankings. It also indicates the various status-roles attached to the size of holdings and the rights to use or control the land.

Since tenure rank determined the socio-economic status of the farmer, it directly influenced the conditions of marriage and education. With the pressure of an increasing farm population on a small cultivated area and the lack of opportunities for advancing on the "agricultural ladder," social mobility was extremely limited. It can be safely said that the various sanctions of pre-reform tenure arrangements more or less prevented farm people from leaving the groups into which they were born.

II. Demographic Position

Egypt's first attempt in modern times to make an official population census was in 1882. This census is usually regarded as disqualified for comparison with the later censuses because of a serious undercount. The second census was taken, after fifteen years, in 1897. Censuses were taken after that every tenth year, in 1907, 1917, 1927, 1937, and 1947. A census was scheduled for 1957 but was never taken.

The census returns are not sufficiently accurate for comparison: there appear to be considerable differences in the content of the schedules and variations in the degree of accuracy. The general opinion is that the 1927 and 1937 censuses underestimated the population, and that the 1947 census overestimated the population.[15] The data available in the census returns, however, are used here in spite of their inaccuracy or lack of uniformity.

AGE AND SEX COMPOSITION

The age composition of the population showed two striking features. One was the low proportion of the population of working age (from fifteen to sixty-four years old); this proportion was 57 per cent of the total population in 1947. The other was the high ratio of children to adult population, and hence the high dependency ratio. There were sixty-nine children under fifteen per one hundred persons fifteen to sixty-four years old according to the 1947 census.[16] It is true that in Egypt children are commonly engaged in productive work before the age of fifteen years, and are thus not wholly dependent, but their productive contribution is undoubtedly less, on the average, than that of adult workers. Further, this contribution is made in large part at the expense of the education which they need in order to help raise Egypt's level of productive efficiency and economic development.

As to the sex composition, the population is normally divided about equally between the sexes. The 1947 returns show a slight preponderance of females, but in view of the margin of error in the census, little significance can be attributed to this difference.

OCCUPATIONAL COMPOSITION

The majority of the Egyptian population draws its livelihood from agriculture. However, the number of people in industrial occupations has been increasing steadily since 1937. There has been also a gratifying growth in the professional occupations. The number of physicians and dentists rose from 3,700 in 1937 to 6,300 in 1947. That of chemists and pharmacists increased from 1,200 to 1,600; of school teachers from 35,300 to 52,100; of writers and journalists from 1,200 to 8,200; of lawyers from 3,400 to 4,700; of clerks from 102,300 to 127,900; and of engineers from 8,400 to 15,800.

RURAL-URBAN COMPOSITION

The urban area is comprised of the Governorates of Cairo, Alexandria, Canal, Suez, Damietta, the fifteen provincial capitals, and the district seats. The rural population lives in the villages and in smaller communities—Esbas, Nag's, and Kafrs.

Most of the Egyptian people live in rural areas, but the rural-urban distribution has been continuously changing. In 1947, the urban population represented 31 per cent of the total, against 25 per cent in 1937. This increase in urbanization may be attributed to the war, since migration from rural to urban communities was greatly accelerated by the opportunities for employment provided by the Allied Armies.

NATIONALITY COMPOSITION

Nearly all of the people in Egypt are Egyptian citizens; the foreign population is numerically insignificant. In 1947, foreign residents amounted only to 0.8 per cent of the total population. Their occupational distribution differed significantly from that of the Egyptians. Only 1 per cent of the foreigners were engaged in agriculture, against 59 per cent of the Egyptians; 24 per cent worked in industry and transport against 10 per cent; 22 per cent in commerce and finance against 6 per cent; and 20 per cent in services against 5 per cent. The predominance of foreigners was most marked in the higher levels of finance, trade, and industry. Since 1923, however, Egyptian participation in industry and trade has increased as a result of the various measures taken by the government to Egyptianize business.

EDUCATIONAL COMPOSITION

When Egypt became independent in 1922, and consequently took over the control of education from the British, almost 90 per cent of the people were illiterate. Elementary education was available to only 10 per cent of the population, secondary education was very limited, and there was no state university. The 1923 constitution provided for compulsory free education between the ages of six and twelve. In 1944, a law was enacted for mass education under government supervision. This law organized the campaign against illiteracy beyond the elementary school age. In 1950, a law providing free public education through secondary schools was enacted.

The intensity of these efforts may be gauged from the fact that during the past forty years, the school population rose from 324,000 to 2,750,000, and the budget for education rose from £E 1,600,000 to £E 39,000,000. The number of public schools at all educational levels increased to 9,400, and four state universities were instituted. The percentage of literate population, although still low, has more than doubled. In 1947, 22.8 per cent of the population as a whole were literate, 32.8 per cent of the males and 12.8 per cent of the females.

POPULATION GROWTH

In the decade after 1897, Egypt experienced a rapid growth of population, the annual rate being 1.6 per cent. After 1907 the increase continued at a lower annual rate of 1.3 per cent. During the period from 1917 to 1927, the annual rate of increase declined to 1.1 per cent. But after 1937, the rate increased to 1.9 per cent, mainly because of the gain of births over deaths and the better counting in the latter census. The recent annual increase amounts to 2.2 per cent, and, if it were to continue, the population would double within thirty-five years. The figures in Table III indicate the population increase in Egypt since the first reliable census.

At present Egypt is one of the most densely populated countries in the world. The total population (estimated at about 22,500,000 in 1954) occupies a relatively small proportion of the land area, for though the country covers 386,198 square miles, 96.5 per cent of this area is uninhabitable desert. The tiny inhabitable area is 13,590 square miles of space consisting of the Nile Valley, the Delta, and a few scattered oases. The average population density of the inhabited area was about 1,650 persons per square mile in 1954.

In studying the reasons for an actual growth in numbers, three important factors must be taken into account: migration, fertility, and mortality.

Migration. There is practically no emigration from Egypt, for Egyptians are greatly attached to their land. Few ever leave except

TABLE III

Annual Rates of Population Increase,
Egypt, 1882-1955

Years	Population (000's)	Average annual increase per cent
Census of		
1882	6,804	---
1897	9,715	2.9
1907	11,287	1.6
1917	12,751	1.3
1927	14,218	1.1
1937	15,933	1.2
1947	19,022	1.9
Mid year Estimate		
1948	19,494	2.2
1949	19,888	2.1
1950	20,393	2.5
1951	20,872	2.3
1952	21,473	2.9
1953	21,987	2.2
1954(1)	22,460	2.2
1955(1)	22,934	2.2

Source: Statistical Pocket Year-Book, 1955
(1) Preliminary estimates

to study or to travel, and they usually return. On the other hand, immigration into Egypt is very slight; foreigners in Egypt are numerically negligible. In 1927, only 1.6 per cent of the Egyptian population had been born outside the country; by 1937 this figure had declined to 1.2 per cent. In 1947, foreigners constituted 0.8 per cent of the total population and were concentrated in Alexandria, Cairo, and the main cities of Lower Egypt.

With regard to internal migration, two main movements within the country could be observed: from Upper to Lower Egypt, and from the villages to the towns and cities. The movement from Upper to Lower Egypt may be attributed to strong economic inducements offered by Egyptian industry, which is concentrated in Lower Egypt. Then too, Upper Egypt, with an average crop area of 0.47 feddan per inhabitant, is more densely populated than Lower Egypt, for which the corresponding figure is 0.64.

The movement from the villages to the towns and cities was greatly accelerated during the war. The five governorates were the center of immigration. Their population rose from 2,249,000 in 1937 to 3,416,000 in 1947. Most of the increase reflected a movement to the cities from the villages. In 1947, about 19 per cent of the population lived in seven cities with a population of 100,000 or more.

From this brief discussion it can be seen that migration can be quickly disposed of as a factor in the growth of Egypt's population.[17] The factors affecting the growth continue to be fertility and mortality.

Fertility. The crude birth rates, as shown in Table IV, mostly exceed 43 per thousand population and indicate a very high fertility. Between 1941 and 1944 the rates declined because of the war. Over the years the rates have fluctuated considerably, but no clear trend can be observed. Fertility ratios, however, seem to indicate a slight decline: the ratio of children under the age of five fell from 700 per thousand females ages fifteen to forty-nine in 1897 to 546 in 1947, a drop of 154 points per thousand in fifty years. The ratios of married women of childbearing age to the total number of women also indicate a slight reduction in the percentage of married women, from 79.4 in 1907 to 74.7 in 1947.

The explanation of the high level of fertility in Egypt may be found in the socio-psychological factors which characterize Egyptian society. The desire to have children is strong among both men and women. The men desire to have children, especially boys, to carry on their names and to increase the earning power of the family. The women like to have children, especially boys, to feel secure with their husbands and to be safe from divorce. The average age at marriage is low, and childbearing is regarded as a moral duty. Where illiteracy and poverty prevail, contraception is unknown, and the family expects a child every year or two.

The explanation of the high fertility rate may be sought also in the absence of the factors which, in other countries, have contributed to a declining rate. Thus, industrialization, urbanization, and a rising standard of living are generally considered to have been the underlying factors associated with the historical decline of birth rates in European countries. These factors have led to a change in the social status of women, to greater costs of rearing a family, to the desire of parents to have their children well educated, to the postponement of marriage, and to the practice of birth control after marriage.

It has been argued that polygyny among the Moslems is a common

TABLE IV

Selected Vital Rates,* Egypt, 1920-51

Year	Birth Rate	Death Rate	Natural Increase	Infant Mortality	Still-Births
1920	42.2	28.0	14.2	137	11.7
1921	41.8	25.0	16.8	133	12.2
1922	43.1	25.1	18.0	140	11.4
1923	43.1	25.8	17.3	143	10.2
1924	43.8	24.9	18.9	150	9.3
1925	43.5	26.5	17.0	155	8.8
1926	44.2	26.7	17.5	146	8.2
1927	44.0	25.2	18.8	152	8.1
1928	43.6	26.3	17.3	151	7.5
1929	44.8	27.6	16.2	159	7.4
1930	45.4	24.9	20.5	151	7.5
1931	44.5	26.6	17.9	160	7.3
1932	42.5	28.5	14.0	174	7.6
1933	43.8	27.5	16.3	162	7.4
1934	42.2	27.8	14.4	166	7.3
1935	41.3	26.4	14.9	161	7.1
1936	44.2	28.8	15.4	164	7.6
1937	43.4	27.1	16.3	165	7.8
1938	43.2	26.3	16.9	163	7.3
1939	42.0	25.9	16.1	161	7.7
1940	41.3	26.3	15.0	162	7.7
1941	40.4	25.7	14.7	150	7.3
1942	37.6	28.3	9.3	168	7.2
1943	38.7	27.7	11.0	160	7.3
1944	39.8	26.0	13.8	157	7.6
1945	42.7	27.7	15.0	153	7.7
1946	41.2	25.0	16.2	141	7.0
1947	43.8	21.4	22.4	127	7.1
1948	42.7	20.4	22.3	139	6.9
1949	41.8	20.6	21.2	135	7.0
1950	44.4	19.1	25.3	130	6.0
1951	44.7	19.3	25.4	129	7.9

* Rates are per 1000 population

Source: Annuaire Statistique, 1951-54

custom which may be associated with the fertility rate in Egypt. Polygynous households, however, represented only 3.1 per cent of the total households in 1937, and 3.7 per cent in 1947. From these figures it is clear that the influence of practicing polygyny in Egypt is of little importance.

Mortality. Not only does fertility affect the growth of Egypt's population, but also mortality, since the growth is finally determined by the excess of births over deaths.

It is clear, as shown in Table IV, that Egypt has high crude death rates. There has been, however, a distinct decline in these rates since the post-war years. The application of new methods of epidemic control, the improvement of sanitation, and the development of public health facilities may continue to bring the death rates well below their present level.

It is important, however, to study death rates of various age groups, for at some ages the mortality is much higher than at others. As in the case of Egypt, if the population happens to be composed largely of persons at ages having high death rates, the general rate for all ages also will be high. Egypt's specific death rates, by age, indicate that the biggest loss in actual numbers is among the children under five years. The rates of the older age groups represent relatively few people and have little influence on the general rate.

The high mortality in Egypt may be explained in several ways. First, there is poverty with its normal concomitants of malnutrition and infectious diseases. There is also the high percentage of illiteracy, ranging in most rural areas between 80 and 90 per cent. There is, finally, the lack of adequate medical care. However, several steps have been and are being taken to increase health facilities; in 1950 there were seven hundred health institutions against forty-five in 1922. The number of general hospitals increased from nineteen in 1922 to one hundred in 1950, and free treatment is being given in all government health institutions. Further progress is held up by the lack of qualified medical personnel. As reported in 1955 there were 7,061 doctors, 573 dentists, and 1,711 pharmacists, but most of these trained people work in large cities.

POPULATION AND RESOURCES

The size of the population and its rate of growth are important elements in the complex of social and economic factors which affect the welfare of the people in any area. Population is an especially important factor in rural areas where most of the people depend upon the land for their livelihood and where the level of living is related to the amount of land available for cultivation per capita. In particular, the population factor is most important in densely populated agricultural areas where it is not easy either to extend the area of land under cultivation or to increase yields per unit of labor on the land already being cultivated. In these circumstances, population growth may constitute an obstacle to economic and social development.[18]

Egypt has been chiefly an agricultural country since the earliest historical recording, and it may remain so for a considerable time. On a cultivated area consisting of six million feddans, about sixteen million people live and depend on agriculture as their only means of livelihood. With the total population estimated at 22,500,000 in 1954, every feddan of arable land must support 3.8 persons. Despite the fertility of the land, the abundance of water for irrigation, and the suitability of the climate, the cultivated area can by no means satisfy the needs of the people.

The surplus population on the land is estimated officially to be five million, including dependents, or 30 per cent of the agricultural population. Should the present trend in population growth continue, Egypt by the end of this century will be facing a situation wherein every feddan of arable land must support ten people. A population of this size appears to be impossible to maintain, even when taking into account foreseeable improvements in agricultural methods, possible expansion of the cultivated area, intensification of agricultural production, and promotion of new industries.[19]

It is nothing new to state, therefore, that the principal problem facing Egypt is the rapid increase in the population as compared with the slow increase in the area of cultivated land. The figures in Table V indicate that during the fifty years from 1897 to 1947, the cultivated area increased by 14 per cent, the crop area increased by 35 per cent, and the population increased by 96 per cent. Accordingly, the cultivated area per head and the crop area per head decreased by 40 per cent and 31 per cent, respectively. The increase in crop production was also at a slower rate than the increase in the

TABLE V

Population, Crop Area, and Cultivated Area, Egypt, 1897-1947

	1897	1907	1917	1927	1937	1947
Population (millions)	9.7	11.3	12.8	14.2	15.9	19.0
Area of crop (millions of feddans)	6.8	7.6	7.8	8.6	8.5	9.2
Area of crop per head (feddan)	0.70	0.67	0.61	0.61	0.53	0.48
Area of cultivated land (millions of feddans)	5.1	5.4	5.3	5.5	5.3	5.8
Area of cultivated land per head (feddans)	0.52	0.48	0.41	0.39	0.33	0.31

Source: _Annuaire Statistique_, 1951-1954

population. During the thirty-five years from 1915 to 1950, crop production increased by 32 per cent, while the population increased by 64 per cent.

At the present time, the existing cultivated area is used to capacity and with high efficiency. On most of the land two and even three crops a year can be raised. Yields are high, the cotton yield being the world's highest. Maize yields are as high as the United States, and wheat yields exceed the European average.[20] Because the population on the land is increasing faster than the crop production, the high level of productivity is accompanied by a very low productivity of labor. Gross and net output per feddan are extremely high, while output per man is extremely low.

Estimates of the Egyptian national income show that in 1953 the average gross agricultural output per feddan amounted to £E 63 and the average net output per feddan to £E 45. Net income per head of active agricultural population amounted to £E 34 and after deduction of rent it amounted to £E 25.[21]

The decrease in agricultural returns per head of the population led to a noticeable shortage in foodstuffs. Egypt, although becoming a net importer on a large scale of cereals, meat, animals, and fruits, was not able to provide sufficient foodstuffs for the minimum standard of necessary nutrition. According to the food balance sheet of 1951-52, the average share per head per day was one hundred calories below the minimum. The most serious shortage lay in animal protein, which is of great value to children and to expectant and nursing mothers. Because of the high fertility rate and the large proportion of children under fifteen years of age, the shortage in animal protein constituted a serious problem in Egypt. The problem became more pronounced because the movement toward urbanization and industrialization changed the tastes, needs, and attitudes of the people. While they lived in the villages, they were usually satisfied with food consisting mostly of bread, cheese, and vegetables. When they moved to the cities, they fell into the habits of urban dwellers as much as their means allowed, and began to consume more meat and fruits.[22]

CHAPTER III

The Agrarian Reform Law of 1952

I. Factors Contributing to the Enactment of the Law

EGYPT has become one of the most densely populated regions in the world. The rural population has suffered from severe underemployment on the land, and tenure arrangements have produced a large group of landless peasants depending on agriculture for their livelihood by working as laborers or tenants. Because of their large numbers and because land ownership was concentrated in the hands of a few, their bargaining position became too weak to oppose the severe terms imposed by the landlords. Laborers were forced to accept meager wages and tenants had to pay exorbitant rents. As a result, the level of living for the majority of the farm population was extremely low.

Although this low level of living created an urgent need to carry out land reform, there were other contributory factors which led to a sincere desire and determination on the part of the revolutionary government to enforce the Agrarian Reform Law in Egypt. These factors included political instability, failure of previous land-reform attempts, influence of foreign ideas, and the Army Revolution.

POLITICAL INSTABILITY

Between 1923 and 1952, Egypt passed through a period of political instability resulting from conflicting interests among the powers dominating the political scene. There was the King, Farouk I, who determined to govern as well as to rule. There were several political parties with contradicting policies. The Ittihad, or Unionist party, represented the "King's friends." The Wafd party represented militant nationalism and the desire for independence. The Liberal Constitutionalists, the Shaabists, and the Saadists were parties formed by successive splits from the Wafd party. They differed in that they were willing to compromise with the British and were more accommodating in their relations with the Monarchy. Finally, above the King and the political parties, was the British Residency, which often had the last word.[1]

Any conflict between the King or the British on the one hand, and the political party in power on the other, ended in the resignation or dismissal of that Government, the dissolution of Parliament, and the suspension or modification of the Constitution. During the period from 1923 to 1951, thirty-one different cabinets were in power and most of these were reshuffled several times during their short terms. The climax came in 1952 when five cabinets were formed in the first six months of that year.

FAILURE OF PREVIOUS REFORM ATTEMPTS

The political power of the landlords in Egypt was such that it was difficult to enact any legislation that would have an adverse effect on their traditional rights.

Several land-reform measures had been introduced to the Parliament, but all were defeated overwhelmingly. In 1945, a bill prohibiting individual acquisition of more than one hundred feddans was introduced. In 1948 the National Progress Association presented to the Senate a comprehensive land-reform program including land reclamation, protection of ownership from fragmentation, maximum limit on individual ownership, ceiling on rents, and floors on daily wages.[2] This proposal was rejected on the grounds that changes in land tenure should come about without any government intervention, and that tenure group relationships should be left to customary local practices and prevailing conventions. In 1950 a bill was introduced to the Parliament for the breaking up, with compensation, of all holdings over fifty feddans. In the same year, another bill provided that newly reclaimed agricultural land owned by the government should be sold only to peasants with holdings under two feddans.

All of these measures were rejected, and the most that could be wrung out of the landlord-dominated Parliament was a law requiring owners of large estates to provide better housing and social services for their tenants. Dr. Ahmed Hussein, the former Ambassador of Egypt to the United States, said in an address delivered at Washington, D.C.:

> The Parliament consisted mainly of these feudal lords. . . . Their interests and their interests alone were served, and any progressive legislation for the welfare of the masses was undermined. For example, when I was in the Department of Social Affairs in 1943, I tried to introduce a bill for agrarian reform with the object of creating minimum wage for its laborers. I kept on trying to have this bill passed by Parliament for nine years, but in vain. As a Cabinet Minister, I presented a bill to fix minimum wages in agriculture and industry that would secure the basic needs of poorer families. I was fought until I was so disgusted that I resigned.[3]

INFLUENCE OF FOREIGN IDEAS

Between 1950 and 1952, land tenure problems of underdeveloped countries and land reform as a solution were very much in the air internationally. The Economic and Social Council of the United Nations adopted a resolution which recommended that "governments institute appropriate land reforms in the interest of landless farmers and those with small and medium-sized holdings."[4] The Council further indicated the broad range of objectives that must be sought in a genuine land-reform program: efficient size of farm units, security of tenure on land, the right of men who work the land to own it, clear titles to land and water, adequate credit at reasonable rates, more efficient marketing methods, and equitable taxes on land and its produce. The Council also suggested the development of farm co-operatives for cultivating, marketing, and processing agricultural products; the establishment of small-scale cottage industries; and the promotion of literacy programs and extension services.

Before the Twelfth Council session of the Food and Agriculture Organization in Rome, Under-Secretary of Agriculture, Clarence J. McCormick, stated:

> Land reform in its broadest interpretation deeply affects security in the world today. . . . The United States Government intends giving encouragement and assistance to land reform. . . . We shall do so in both planning and administration of our foreign economic and technical assistance program, and we will also lend other practical assist-

> ance to desirable land reforms in addition to the economic and technical assistance programs. . . . Furthermore, we shall take every opportunity to support and encourage desirable land reform programs through all appropriate international agencies.[5]

At the Conference on World Land Tenure Problems in Madison, Wisconsin, delegations from fifty nations, including Egypt, discussed freely the land tenure problems prevailing in their countries. Land reform was presented as a genuine program for solving these problems and fostering national development. Willard L. Thorp, Former United States Assistant Secretary of State for Economic Affairs, expressed the United States' point of view as follows:

> The important question is: How can this movement toward land reform be encouraged? . . . It is basically the job for the people of each nation. They must want it. They must see the importance of land problems to their own national development. They must become aware of the promise which land reform holds for their future. . . . They must create a political environment favorable to the development of an improved land system. The United States has no special responsibility for and no unique competence in solving land problems the world over. . . . We have, however, encouraged and supported the land reform programs of other nations. We will continue that encouragement and support.[6]

Since World War II, many countries have undertaken reform measures for limiting land ownership and redistributing the large estates among the landless peasants. The extent of these measures varied from one country to another, according to the prevailing economic, social, and political conditions. Of special interest to Egyptians were the land-reform measures undertaken in neighboring countries. In Turkey, a law passed in 1945 set a maximum limit of ownership at five hundred hectares and provided for the redistribution of 423,000 hectares among peasants. In Iran the Crown (Shah) land in three thousand villages was divided in 1951 among the peasants who were actually cultivating the land. Italy, in 1950, enacted the Sila Law, which provided for expropriation of properties over three hundred hectares, and the Stralcio Law, which combined the farm income with the intensity of cultivation as a criterion for expropriation. India, in 1949-1951, enacted land-reform laws to abolish the Zamindari system of absentee landlords and redistributed their estates among the landless.[7]

THE ARMY REVOLUTION

The pressure of overpopulation, the increasing underemployment on the land, the unwillingness of the ruling class to make any contribution to the well-being of the people, and the influence of foreign ideas all combined to bring about the disillusionment and disgust of the Egyptian people. Four alternative courses appeared to confront Egypt: reform, repression, foreign occupation, or revolution. There appeared to be neither the will nor the means for reform. Successful repression depended on a strengthening of the loyalty and efficiency of the Army, the police, and the administrative services. Foreign occupation—British occupation—was likely only in the event of a complete breakdown of law and order. Revolution depended on the emergence of a revolutionary organization.

On January 25, 1952, the situation reached a crisis when at the Canal Zone, British forces, alleging harassment by guerillas, surrounded in their barracks a battalion of Egyptian police and attacked them with tanks and light artillery. The news of this event caused a serious outbreak of violence in Cairo, starting with the police and extending to the hungry mob. Although the outbreak was in origin anti-British, it soon developed into a wild general disorder, in the course of which many of Cairo's restaurants, bars, movie theatres, and luxury shops were burned. Hunger, desperation, and the hatred of the poor for the rich appeared to be the dominating passions released on that day. Order was restored late in the afternoon by the Army, for the situation had passed out of the control of the police.

The Army, by its successful intervention, had demonstrated that it held the key to the situation, and it became obvious that the Army was gravely discontented with the Palace. At that time, two of Lenin's three prerequisites for a revolutionary situation existed in Egypt. There was widespread discontent, and there was governmental impotence. The third prerequisite, an organization capable of taking advantage of the first two, had yet to emerge.

On the early morning of July 23, 1952, a few battalions of army troops captured the Army General Headquarters, and marched on Cairo. Armed cars and tanks guarded public buildings and main squares. Bomber and fighter planes flew to protect the entire country. By dawn the revolutionary forces were in complete command of the capital and its broadcasting system. The coup was engineered by an army officers' group which had begun to take shape in 1945 as the "Free Officers Organization."

In the few days that followed the coup, the Government was dismissed, and the King was ordered to abdicate and leave the country. Arrangements were made for a new government, and a Regency Council was established to represent the King's infant son. The decision to undertake land reform was announced and the main lines of the Agrarian Reform Law were prepared. It soon became apparent that the "Free Officers" had not only achieved a successful coup, but also aspired to generate a social revolution.

The Agrarian Reform Law was not immediately put into force by the first cabinet formed after the Revolution. It later became apparent that Prime Minister Aly Mahir, under the pretext of studying the experiences of other countries, was in reality opposing the law. On September 7, 1952, the Cabinet was removed and the "Free Officers" decided to take over the government. On the following day, they began to put in effect the Agrarian Reform Law.

II. Objectives of the Law

The explanatory note by Dr. El-Emery, Minister of Finance, on the Agrarian Reform Law stated the objectives of the Law in the following terms:

> The crux of our problem lies in the low standard of living among the majority of Egyptians, which is the result of the low level of national income in comparison to the population, and the failure of increased production to provide a suitable standard of living for the steadily growing population. . . .
>
> The Egyptian economy suffers from one shortcoming that up to now has thwarted its rapid growth. This shortcoming is the marked tendency on the part of the people to invest

> their savings in arable land, the area of which has not increased with the increase of demand. . . .
>
> To prepare the ground for rapid economic development, . . . one of the chief objectives of the proposed land reform is to devote every new investment to land reclamation and to mining, industrial, and commercial projects. . . .
>
> Such, in brief, is the economic side of our problem, and although it alone constitutes sufficient justification for amending the arable land ownership system, there are social justifications which must not be overlooked because the distribution of wealth in Egyptian rural districts is at variance with any concept of justice. . . . The unequal distribution of agricultural wealth gave rise to social evils. . . . One of the worst effects of these evils is the enslavement by a minority of big landlords of the peasants and the direction of the country's general policy according to their personal interests, which in no way conform with the principles of democracy. . . . The time has now come for reforms in Egypt to be carried out with a view to rebuilding Egyptian society on a new basis that would secure for every individual a free and honorable life, close the wide gap between landowners, and remove the deep-rooted class barriers with their attendant social and political unrest.[8]

This statement indicates the diversity in the objectives of the Agrarian Reform Law, economic as well as social and political objectives. The economic objectives aim at raising the level of living through the acceleration of economic development. The social objectives aim at abolishing the social evils that had resulted from the unequal distribution of agricultural wealth. The political objectives are implicit in the formulation of the economic and social objectives. Phrases in the explanatory note, such as, "to prepare the ground for rapid economic development," or "rebuilding Egyptian society on a new basis," pertain to political aspects of the Law. These phrases imply measures to prevent the minority of big landlords from directing the general policy of the country according to their personal interests, and also imply measures which elevate the peasants to a state where they can exercise their rights and duties in a democratic political life.

It is clear that these groups of objectives are closely interrelated and cannot be disassociated. The Higher Committee for Agrarian Reform, however, operationally classifies the objectives of the Law into long range objectives, and objectives directly linked with the welfare of those engaged in agriculture.[9]

The long range objectives are: (1) to direct every new investment into industrial and commercial activities by fixing a maximum limit for land ownership, (2) to encourage land reclamation by permitting holders of fallow or desert land to own as much as they wish to attempt to reclaim, (3) to create from the peasants a new class of small landowners who are not dependent on their landlords for their livelihoods and political opinions, and (4) to prevent any further fragmentation of the small-size holdings.

Objectives directly linked with the welfare of those engaged in agriculture are: (1) to abolish the feudal system by expropriating the land in excess of a maximum ownership limit, (2) to return the land to its tillers by redistributing the expropriated land among those who actually cultivate it, (3) to improve living conditions of farm people by establishing co-operative organizations for the small owners, (4) to provide for a more equitable division of income between landowners and tenants by fixing a maximum limit for land rent, (5) to provide security for tenants by fixing a minimum term for land leases, and (6) to insure the rights of agricultural laborers by fixing their wages and permitting them to form trade unions.

The objectives of the Agrarian Reform Law reflect the complexity of the problems which were and are encountered. The classification of these objectives into economic, social, and political objectives shows how the law affects all aspects of rural life. The distinction between long range objectives and objectives directly linked with those engaged in agriculture shows how the law embraces the various strata of the farm population.

III. Provisions of the Law

EXPROPRIATION OF LAND IN EXCESS OF TWO HUNDRED FEDDANS

The law sets two hundred feddans as a maximum limit of ownership and empowers the government to requisition any land holdings in excess of this maximum limit within a period of five years.[10] Exceptions have been made for industrial companies with holdings necessary for industrial development, and for societies or individuals engaged in the reclamation of land for the purpose of its ultimate sale. The landowner may within a period of five years after the enactment of the law transfer the ownership of his land in excess of the maximum limit in the following manner: to his children at a maximum rate of fifty feddans per child, provided that the total transferred to his children does not exceed one hundred feddans; to farmers owning fewer than five feddans, provided that their ownership thereafter does not exceed ten feddans; or to graduates of Agricultural Institutes who own fewer than twenty feddans, provided that the land so disposed of must be orchards and in holdings of not fewer than ten and not more than twenty feddans.

COMPENSATION TO EXPROPRIATED LAND OWNERS

Compensation is paid to landowners for land expropriated by the government in the form of nominal Treasury Bonds bearing 3 per cent interest and redeemable within thirty years. The rate of compensation equals seventy times the basic land tax plus the value of fixed and mobile installations and trees. If the land expropriated by the Law is mortgaged, the debt is deducted from the compensation.

DISTRIBUTION OF REQUISITIONED LAND

The requisitioned land is to be distributed by the government in lots of not fewer than two feddans and not more than five feddans each. A person eligible to acquire land must be an Egyptian, of age, not convicted of any dishonorable crime, working in agriculture, and must own fewer than five feddans.

The plan of distribution is based on the assumption that the land belongs to its tillers. Priority in acquiring land is given to those who actually cultivate the land, then to peasants having the largest families in the village, then to those possessing less wealth among their fellow villagers, and finally to non-residents of the village.

The price of land distributed to farmers is based on the rate of compensation paid by the government to the original owners, plus 15 per cent for expropriation and distribution expenses, plus 3 per cent annual interest rate. The price of each portion of distributed land is to be paid by the new farmer-owner in thirty equal annual installments.

ESTABLISHMENT OF AGRICULTURAL CO-OPERATIVE SOCIETIES

Farmers who acquire the requisitioned land are obliged to join co-operative societies established to render agricultural and social services to the members. The societies organize the cultivation of land, provide the members with loans, seeds, fertilizers, and machinery, market the principal products and crops, and collect the annual installments of the price of the land. The co-operative societies perform these functions under the supervision of an official chosen by the Higher Committee for Agrarian Reform.

LIMITATIONS ON DIVIDING AGRICULTURAL LAND

Should there be an occasion to divide agricultural land into lots of fewer than five feddans, whether through sale, exchange, inheritance, or through any other means, the parties concerned must come to an agreement as to which of them shall assume ownership of the land, and that person shall compensate the others for their shares. Should there be disagreement among the parties as to who shall retain the land, the matter shall be submitted to a Summary Court. Preference in such matters shall be given to the one working in agriculture. Should all the parties satisfy this condition, lots shall be drawn among them. In case no one of the parties concerned is in a position to buy the land as a whole, the Court shall order the land to be sold at public auction.

REGULATION OF LANDLORD-TENANT RELATIONSHIP

The Law provides that no land can be rented except to a tenant who will farm the land himself. The rent of agricultural land must not exceed seven times the basic tax assessed upon the land. In case of crop-sharing rent, the owner's share must not exceed one-half the crop after deduction of all expenses. Agricultural land may not be leased for fewer than three years and the contract must be in writing, regardless of the amount involved.

RIGHTS OF AGRICULTURAL LABORERS

The Law provides that the wages of agricultural laborers in various agricultural districts should be fixed every year by a committee appointed by the Minister of Agriculture. This provision does not apply to laborers who perform duties in the public interest according to special laws.

The Law also gives agricultural laborers the right to form trade unions to further their common interests.

IV. Execution of the Law

ADMINISTRATION

The administrative machinery of land reform is composed of the Higher Committee for Agrarian Reform, the Executive Agency, and the Judicial Committee.

The Higher Committee was established to supervise the implementation and management of the scheme. The Minister of State for Agrarian Reform is the presiding officer; other members are the Minister of Agriculture, the President of the State Council, the Under Secretaries of Agriculture, Social Affairs, Public Works, and Finance and Economy, the Executive Director of Agrarian Reform, the Chancellor of the Agrarian Reform Legal Department, and five others appointed by the President of the Republic.

The Higher Committee is an independent body, with a separate budget and its own rules of procedure, which govern all budgetary, financial, and administrative matters. The Committee has the authority to interpret the provisions of the Agrarian Reform Law, to fix the amount of money needed to increase agricultural production on the land requisitioned and distributed, and to participate in any project for improving the conditions of the farmers.

The Executive Agency carries out the various operations of the land-reform program. The Agency is comprised of several specialized departments for land requisition, land distribution, land survey, farm management, engineering, co-operation, technical research, press, legislation, and general administration.

The Judicial Committee handles all disputes arising between landowners and the Higher Committee and is composed of a Counsellor from the National Courts, a technical official from the Council of State, a member of the Higher Committee for Agrarian Reform, and a representative from the Survey Department. The decisions of the Judicial Committee are subject to the ratification of the Higher Committee.

FINANCE

When the Agrarian Reform Law became effective, the Higher Committee was established within the Ministry of Agriculture and began operations with a weak financial arrangement subject to governmental routine and rules of finance. As a result many financial problems accumulated. To free the Committee from these stifling governmental regulations, a decree was issued providing it with independent identity and a special budget.

Since then, the Higher Committee for Agrarian Reform has been able to strengthen its position and has become financially self-sufficient. Financing of land-reform programs was facilitated by the success of the Committee in leasing the requisitioned land, and acquiring, without compensation, the 178,000 feddans confiscated from the descendants of Mohamed Aly. The confiscated land was distributed by the Higher Committee at the same price rates charged for any other expropriated land. By the end of 1955, the Higher Committee had a net profit of £E 2,754,800.[11]

REQUISITION PROCEDURE

The law governing limitation of land ownership affected 1,789 landowners, and the total area declared liable to expropriation amounted to 656,736 feddans. This land was requisitioned by the Higher Committee during the five-year period specified by the Law. Violent opposition on the part of the big landlords against the requisition procedures was expected and prepared for by the authorities concerned. Contravention occurred, however, only in the case of one big landlord in Upper Egypt, who with a band of retainers attacked the prefecture at the town of Maghagha. He was then arrested, tried by a military court, and condemned to penal servitude for life. Later, he was released. Apart from this instance, the requisition procedure was carried out without any hostility or force.

THE TRANSITIONAL PERIOD

In executing the Agrarian Reform Law, a transitional period occurred between the requisition and distribution of the land. The Higher Committee was entrusted with the management of the requisitioned land in order to undertake the measures necessary prior to the distribution.

During this transitional period, the Committee rented the land to its previous tenants on a temporary basis for one year at the rate of seven times the basic land tax. A representative, assisted by a number of agriculturists, was assigned to each land-reform zone to supervise management of the requisitioned land and to provide its tenants with all kinds of material and technical assistance so that the level of production would not decline. In the meantime, preliminary studies on land productivity and the socio-economic conditions of the rural population were carried out for the Higher Committee by its social workers, in order to determine the best methods of land distribution.

DISTRIBUTION PROCEDURE

Before distributing the land in any village, the Higher Committee conducted a socio-economic survey of those eligible to acquire land according to the Agrarian Reform Law. This survey covered details on the living conditions of every tenant and his family, the average income per feddan, and the average cost of living for families of different sizes renting land in the village.

The family was defined as: "A group of individuals getting their livelihood from one and the same source on the land, no matter whether members of the group reside in one or more places."[12] The size of holding to be assigned to the new owner was determined so as to provide for him and his family an income exceeding by 10 per cent the cost of their bare necessities. The size of holding was estimated on the basis of the productive capacity per feddan and the average cost of living per family.

The survey of the Higher Committee showed that the cost of living of families living under similar conditions varied according to the number and age of members in each family. Thus, it was decided to emphasize these two factors. The following scale was used in determining the size of holding assigned to each family, with land to be distributed in holdings of not fewer than two and not more than five feddans.[13]

AGE OF MEMBERS	UNIT OF LAND*
Under 7 years	¼ of a unit
From 7 to 14 years	½ of a unit
Over 14 to 21 years	¾ of a unit
Head of family (regardless of age)	1¼ unit

*The average unit equals one-half of a feddan.

In distributing the land in a village, the Higher Committee took into consideration the obligatory application of the three-year system of crop rotation. The land was divided into blocks varying in size, and each block was divided into three equal parts. Owners with land in a block were given land in each part. Each part was then to be sown with a single crop or two related crops. New owners receiving smaller holdings were given land closer to their homes than those receiving bigger holdings. An area of land was left around the village for future expansion.

It was deemed necessary to devise priorities in land distribution, especially since the requisitioned estates varied in their capacity to absorb the people living on them. Some estates were not big enough to provide holdings for all those who were eligible to acquire land according to the Law. First priority in acquiring land was given to tenants renting the land before the enactment of the Agrarian Reform Law on condition that they were continuous cultivators of that land. Next in priority were tenants renting the land after the enactment of the Agrarian Reform Law, provided there was enough land to absorb them. Among these, priority was given according to date of tenancy. Tenants of the year 1952-53 had priority over tenants of 1953-54, and in like manner for each successive year. Last in order of priority (where there was surplus land after the tenants had been absorbed) were the peasants having the largest families among the inhabitants of the village, then the less wealthy among them, and finally, the inhabitants of immediately neighboring villages.

The official figure for land liable to expropriation was 656,736 feddans, but the land actually available for redistribution was less than the area legally liable to expropriation. Many landowners privately sold or transferred parts of their land in excess of the maximum ownership limit. The Higher Committee indicated that 145,000 feddans were thus sold and transferred privately by landowners.[14] Another 156,917 feddans were declared to be fallow land and thus were not subject to immediate requisition.[15] The total land available to the Higher Committee for distribution among small farmers was, therefore, presumably 354,819 feddans.

FORMATION OF CO-OPERATIVE SOCIETIES

Agricultural co-operative societies were formed to secure the benefits of large scale operations and production by grouping the small holdings into big units for cultivation purposes. To these big units, improved technical agricultural methods and machinery were applied to reduce the cost of production as well as to improve it. Crop rotation was practiced to prevent the exhaustion of the soil. Cash loans and cultivation requisites (seeds, fertilizer, machinery, etc.) were provided to protect the members from usurers and black-market merchants. Major crops were sold collectively in order to secure a higher price than could be obtained by the individual farmer.

By June, 1956, there had been established in the land-reform areas 198 co-operative societies, with 51,898 members to whom an area of 177,962 feddans had been distributed. The capital of these co-operatives at that time amounted to £E 183,560.[16]

Chapter IV

The Effect of Land Reform on Rural Communities

In order to examine and evaluate the effect of land reform on rural communities, a matched-area survey was conducted. Three land-reform estates were matched with three Wakf estates in respect to geographical location, cultural background, physical setting, agrarian structure, and structure of rural social systems in 1952.[1]

The three land-reform estates were expropriated from their original owners and distributed in 1953, the first year of land distribution, among small tenants in the area. The estates are located at the northern part of Lower Egypt and include Demera in Dakahlia Province, Zafaran in Kafr El-Sheik Province, and Maania in Behira Province.

The three Wakf estates were selected to serve as control devices against which apparent changes effected by land reform could be examined. These estates also are located at the northern part of Lower Egypt and include Shawa in Dakahlia Province, Beyala in Kafr El-Sheik Province, and Saft Khaled in Behira Province. Because the land in these estates was mortmain property which had been dedicated to religious institutions and for charitable purposes, it was inalienable; it could not be sold, transferred, or mortgaged. It could, however, be exchanged for other property of similar value, and it could be rented. The Ministry of Wakf, which supervised the management of this property, rented the land to small tenants in the area. When the Agrarian Reform Law was enacted, the Wakf estates were exempt from expropriation and distribution measures, and the tenants remained on the land without acquiring its ownership.[2]

The matched-area survey covered the changes effected in the agrarian structure and the structure of rural social systems during the period from 1952 to 1956. The data presented were compiled by the author from the official records and registries of the surveyed estates.

I. Brief Description of the Surveyed Estates

The purpose of the following description is to provide an over-all view of each of the six surveyed estates with emphasis on the agricultural area and how it was used.

THE LAND-REFORM ESTATES

Demera. This estate is located in Dakahlia Province in the north-east section of the Delta. Its agricultural area of 15,383 feddans includes thirteen farms, which were formerly the property of four families. About twelve thousand feddans of this area were owned by the Toson family, relatives of former King Farouk.

Generally speaking, the returns are high from this estate which has almost no fallow or poor land. The former owners were absentee landlords who left the management of the estate to a manager assisted by a staff of accountants. The estate was divided and leased to inhabitants of the area. By checking rent contracts for the year 1951-1952, it was found that 79 per cent of the land was leased directly to small farmers in plots consisting of one to ten feddans. A very few tenants rented larger plots and, in most cases, did not cultivate the land themselves. They either sublet what they rented to small farmers or employed workers to cultivate the land.

Rental values were based on cotton prices. A formula was used fixing a minimum rent at £E 12 per feddan on the basis of a minimum price of cotton at £E 3 per cantar (112 lbs.). For every £E 1 increase in the actual price of cotton over the fixed minimum, the value fixed as a minimum rent was increased by 10 per cent. In 1951-1952, the average annual rent per feddan in the estate was £E 26.40, and the average price of cotton per cantar was £E 15.

The two-year system of crop rotation was usually followed in order to increase as much as possible the area of cultivated cotton, thus extracting the greatest possible income from the land without regard for the depletion of soil fertility or the urgent need of the country for other crops and cereals. Crops raised other than cotton were rice, wheat, corn, and alfalfa.

The estate was expropriated in November, 1952, and land distribution began in July, 1953. By the end of 1956, an area of 11,326 feddans, or 73.6 per cent of the total estate had been distributed among 3,567 farm families in holdings averaging 3.2 feddans. Another 4,025 feddans were assigned to 1,530 farm families on a rental basis at a rate equivalent to seven times the land tax. Although these families were not yet granted land ownership, they enjoyed all the facilities offered to new owners.

Zafaran. This estate is located in Kafr-El-Sheik Province in the north-central section of the Delta. Its total agricultural area of 9,249 feddans consists of seven farms. Most of this area was the property of the Egyptian Government until 1926 when its ownership was transferred to King Foad in exchange for Zafaran Palace at Cairo; hence, the name of the estate. The king divided the estate and leased the land to inhabitants of the area. Because the land was fallow, rental values were estimated after the harvest of the crops according to the production. In the meantime, reclamation projects were under way; by 1942 most of the land had been reclaimed and leased to small farmers in return for a fixed share of the crops—cotton, wheat, rice, corn, and alfalfa.

The estate was expropriated in November, 1952, and land distribution began in July, 1953. By the end of 1956 an area of 4,050 feddans or 43.8 per cent of the estate had been distributed among 1,254 families in holdings averaging 3.2 feddans. Another 4,250 feddans were assigned to 1,272 farmers on a rental basis at seven times the land tax. Most of these farmers were awaiting decisions granting them ownership of the land.

Maania. This estate is located in Behira Province in the west section of the Delta and was formerly the property of the descendants of Prince Mohammed Abdel-Halim. The estate, with an agricultural area of 1,101 feddans, is now a part of Itay El-Baroud land-reform zone which consists of seventeen farms with a total agricultural area of 21,540 feddans.

The land in Maania estate is of average quality, better than that of Zafaran, but less fertile than the land in Demera. The former absentee landlords left the management of the estate to a manager assisted by a staff of accountants. Before 1930 the land was leased to a few rent jobbers who sublet their areas to small farmers. During the depression of the 1930's, crop prices fell sharply and the farmers were unable to pay the rent, which resulted in a great loss to the rent jobbers. Consequently, the manager employed agricultural laborers and farmed the land. After 1938 the land was leased again, but only to small farmers directly in plots of from one to ten feddans. The rent was fixed according to the productivity of the land and was payable in cash. Average rental value per feddan was estimated at £E 24 in 1951-1952. Crops raised included cotton, rice, wheat, corn, and alfalfa.

The estate was expropriated in November, 1952, and land distribution began in July, 1953. By the end of 1956, an area of 815 feddans, or 74 per cent of the estate, had been distributed among 254 farmers in holdings averaging 3.1 feddans. Another 286 feddans were assigned to 141 farmers on a rental basis at seven times the land tax.

THE CONTROL ESTATES

Shawa. This estate is located in Dakahlia Province in the northeast section of the Delta, only a few miles from Demera land-reform estate. Its agricultural area of 14,875 feddans consists of eleven farms. Land productivity, in general, is high because of the fertility of the soil, the abundance of water for irrigation, and the adequacy of drainage facilities.

The estate was mortmain property which had been dedicated by Zinab Hanem, daughter of Mohammed Aly, to religious institutions and for charitable purposes. A staff from the Department of Royal Wakf undertook the management of the estate. The land was leased to inhabitants of the area, mostly in small plots ranging from one to ten feddans. Leases were issued in return for a fixed share of the crops—cotton, wheat, rice, corn, and alfalfa.

After the Egyptian Revolution of 1952, the Department of Royal Wakf was dissolved. The Wakf estates were exempt from expropriation and distribution measures, and their management was transferred to the Ministry of Wakf. Two decrees were issued providing for a four-year extension of rent contracts which expired in 1952. Another decree fixed rents at a rate equivalent to seven times the basic tax assessment on the land.[3]

In accordance with these decrees, the management of Shawa estate was taken over by the Ministry of Wakf, leases were extended until 1956, and rents were fixed at seven times the land tax. The tenants remained on the land without acquiring its ownership. There were

5,836 tenants who rented plots averaging 2.5 feddans at an average annual rent of £E 20.50 per feddan.

Beyala. This estate is located in Kafr El-Sheik Province in the north-central section of the Delta, adjacent to Zafaran land-reform estate. Its total agricultural area of 7,280 feddans consists of four farms. About half of this area is fallow land because of the high percentage of sodium chloride in the soil.

The estate was mortmain property which had been dedicated by Gamila Hanem Khairy to El-Azhar University. A staff from the Department of Royal Wakf undertook the management of the estate until 1952. The land was divided into small plots and leased to inhabitants of the area in return for a fixed share of the crops, and the tenants had the right to choose the plots they liked. Consequently, the fallow land was usually left unrented.

In 1952 the management of the estate was transferred to the Ministry of Wakf, and rents were fixed at seven times the land tax. The last tax assessments were made in 1946 when the land was newly reclaimed and its productivity was low, but by 1952 land productivity had increased, and consequently the new rents were much below the market level.

In 1956 an area of 3,890 feddans was leased to 633 tenants in plots averaging six feddans. About 3,015 feddans were fallow land, and another 230 feddans were cultivated by agricultural laborers for the Ministry of Wakf.

Saft Khaled. This estate is located in Behira Province in the west section of the Delta, a few miles from Maania land-reform estate. Its agricultural area of 5,680 feddans consists of four farms. With the exception of a fallow area of two hundred feddans, the land is of average quality. The estate was mortmain property dedicated by Princess Iyn El-Hayat Ibrahim to industrial education schools. A staff from the Department of Royal Wakf had managed the estate and leased the land in return for a fixed share of the crops. In 1952, the management of the estate was transferred to the Ministry of Wakf. Except for 1,040 feddans leased to four agronomists, the land was rented by small tenants in plots averaging 3.8 feddans.

II. Changes in Agrarian Structure

The term "agrarian structure" is used here to mean the institutional framework of agricultural production and includes: the system under which land is owned, the distribution of land ownership, the system under which land is leased, and the organization of production, credit, and marketing.

Besides limiting to two hundred feddans the amount of land owned by any individual, land reform caused changes in both custom and law regarding land ownership, as shown in the three land-reform estates here discussed. The survey shows that each person who acquired land ownership under the reform had to satisfy certain personal qualifications. First, a nationality qualification: he must be an Egyptian. Second, an age qualification: he must be over twenty-one years old. Third, a moral qualification: he must not have been convicted of any dishonorable crime. Fourth, an occupational qualification: he must be working in agriculture. Fifth, an economic qualification: he must own fewer than five feddans.

Persons who lacked any one of these qualifications were not eligible to own land. For those who did possess these qualifications, the following order of priority in acquiring land ownership was established: tenant-cultivators, inhabitants with the largest families, inhabitants with the least wealth, and finally non-inhabitants of the village. The farmers who acquired land ownership were not allowed to choose the plots which they purchased, and were not permitted to buy fewer than two or more than five feddans. The expropriated estates were divided, and the owners were assigned to the land by the Higher Committee for Agrarian Reform, who also determined the exact size of the holdings purchased according to their distribution plan.

The farmers were not allowed to estimate the value of the land nor to choose the method of payment. The price of land was fixed at a rate equivalent to seventy times the basic land tax plus interest at 3 per cent plus 15 per cent for the cost of administration. The total price was to be paid in equal annual installments over a period of thirty years, and the farmers could not dispose of their land through sale or rent until they had paid for it in full. Moreover, the farmers were obliged to join supervised co-operative societies established for the purpose of organizing the cultivation and use of land and rendering all agricultural and social services to the members. A decision annulling the right of ownership may be issued by the High Committee to any owner who hinders the work of the co-operative society or fails to fulfill any obligation.

These changes in the ownership system should be viewed in relation to the different degrees of control of the land ordinarily inherent in the three tenure ranks—owner, tenant, and agricultural worker. Usually, a farm laborer has no effective voice or freedom of action in the use and disposition of land. Only those who have the jobs for hire can ration out the limited employment and dictate the necessary terms. A tenant, on the other hand, is likely to have more privileges and opportunities than a laborer. During his term of tenancy he can make the decisions of management for himself, his family, and his employees, if he has any. He has a degree of independence and some freedom of action, even though for only limited periods of time. An owner, however, is the master of his domain as long as he maintains his ownership, and when he has the right to bequeath his land to his heirs, his will as to the use of the land may be effective beyond his own lifetime. These usual privileges of ownership are extremely important because they determine the degree to which the owner can use and dispose of his land.[4]

The land-reform owners acquired the title of the land, but they did not obtain the right to exercise their wills on the land. They are not allowed to sell, sublet, or even to farm independently. Although in terms of tenure status, they have more privileges and opportunities than tenants and laborers, they do lack the essential privileges usually accorded landowners. The author has noticed that the term "mullak," which in the Arabic language means "owners," was not used in the official registries to refer to the peasants who acquired land ownership under the reform. Instead, the term "muntafieen," which means "beneficiaries," was commonly used. It is also of interest to note that the peasants did not refer to themselves as "mullak" (owners), but as "mumallakeen El-Islah," which means the recipients of land ownership under the reform.

Actually, the peasants who acquired land ownership under the reform constitute a new tenure class. They are neither owners, tenants, nor agricultural laborers. They are the reform beneficiaries, the recipients of land ownership under the Agrarian Reform Law, and subject to its controls. There is no evidence, however, that any of them would prefer to be tenants again. Available and conclusive evidence indicates that the recipients of land ownership desire to hold on to the land and to remain in their new status. They pointed out to the writer that they and their fathers had held lifelong hopes of acquiring ownership of the land which they cultivate. Now that they have it, they definitely intend to keep it.

DISTRIBUTION OF LAND OWNERSHIP

The control estates were exempt from expropriation and distribution measures, and there was no transfer of land ownership to the operating tenants. By the end of 1956 about 87.5 per cent of the agricultural area in these estates was leased to 7,627 tenants in plots averaging 3.2 feddans. The remainder of the agricultural area was mostly fallow, unrented land.

In the land-reform estates, a major change took place in the ownership-unit structure. Before land reform, the total agricultural area of the three surveyed estates, 25,733 feddans, was owned by fifteen families. After the reform, in 1956, the ownership of 63 per cent of this area was transferred to 5,075 farm families. The average size of ownership-units per family dropped from 1715.5 feddans in 1952 to 3.2 feddans in 1956.

Because the annual installments of the price of land were substantially less than the previous rents, the distribution of land ownership resulted in a change in the distribution of agricultural income. For example, in 1952 the peasant on the Demera estate paid, on the average, £E 26.40 as rent per feddan. Since he has acquired ownership of the land, he has been paying £E 19.90 per feddan in annual installments. The difference which amounts to £E 6.50 per feddan is, in effect, transferred annually from the landlord to the peasant who acquired land ownership. Unless the gross income per feddan remains the same, however, the difference transferred will not represent a corresponding increase in the net income. Furthermore, unless the size of farm also remains the same, there will be no corresponding increase in the total net income of the farmer.

Actually, it was found that the peasants who were renting considerably over five feddans before the reform suffered a decrease in their total net income because they were assigned a smaller farm. These, however, were few in number. The majority of the peasants were renting fewer than five feddans and their total net income has increased since the reform.

The distribution of the expropriated estates, which reduced the average size of ownership-units from 1715.5 feddans to 3.2 feddans, did not reduce the average size of operating units. Before the reform these estates were already divided and leased to small tenants. The transfer of land ownership from the absentee landlords to these tenants neither reduced the scale of operation nor affected the size of operating units. On both control estates and land-reform estates the average size of operating units is exactly the same. On the control estates an area of 24,355 feddans was leased to 7,627 tenants in plots averaging 3.2 feddans. On the land-reform estates an area of 16,191 feddans was distributed among 5,075 farmers in plots also averaging 3.2 feddans.

The distribution of land did not deprive the expropriated estates of the advantages of large scale operations and production since these estates were not actually large producing units. It must be realized, however, that land reform did not solve the problems of uneconomic small-sized farms which characterize the Egyptian agrarian structure.

LAND TENANCY SYSTEM

Before 1952, the small tenants, in both land-reform and control estates, had no security of tenure, because the landlords had the right to expel them or to terminate their leases at any time. The land was leased on a cash basis or in return for a fixed share of the crop. Cash rental values varied from year to year according to the fluctuations in cotton prices. A common agreement regarding sharecropping rent was that the owner (or manager) received a fixed amount of the crop regardless of what the land produced. Sharecropping, therefore, was not a contract between the owner (or manager) to divide the profits of the land, but it was simply a method of reducing labor costs. This method encouraged the rent jobbers who possessed some capital to rent large areas of land, and, instead of farming it themselves, to sublet it to small farmers on a sharecropping basis.

These unsatisfactory tenancy conditions have changed since the Agrarian Reform Law effected the regulation of the landlord-tenant relationship throughout the country.

The survey shows that in both the land-reform and control estates, the tenants have been enjoying a higher degree of security and certainty than before. The uncertainty of leasing was eliminated by assuring the tenant of at least three years on the land, so that he can make more efficient and comprehensive production plans. It was noticed, for example, that most of the tenants who were following the two-year system of crop rotation changed to the three-year system in order to organize crop production and avoid depletion of soil fertility.

Rents under land reform were fixed at a lower rate than before. On Demera estate, average rents dropped from £E 26.40 per feddan in 1951-1952 to £E 22.80 per feddan in 1952-1953, a decrease of 13.6 per cent. On Shawa estate, average rents dropped from £E 25.60 to £E 20.50, a decrease of 20 per cent. On Beyala estate, where taxes on the land were under-assessed, average rents dropped from £E 21.00 in 1951-1952 to £E 11.50 in 1952-1953, a decrease of 45 per cent. This average rose to £E 14.50 after 1953 because the Ministry of Wakf, which manages the estate, has found a way to escape the provisions of the Law. The Ministry leased the land with under-assessed taxes on a sharecropping basis and obliged the tenants to buy its share at a fixed price. Although the Law stipulates that rents should not exceed seven times the basic land tax, the fixed price collected by the Ministry as rent amounted to sixteen times the land tax. This action by the Ministry of Wakf demonstrates how difficult it is to enforce measures for the reduction and control of rents in a country where the cultivated area is limited and the demand for land is steadily rising.

ORGANIZATION OF PRODUCTION, CREDIT, AND MARKETING

One of the most important changes that took place as a result of land reform was the establishment of obligatory, supervised co-operative societies for the new owners. These societies have been introduced to combine the incentives of individual ownership with the technical advantages of large scale operation and production. Land ownership is retained individually, while farming operations are conducted co-operatively.

This system of co-operation is new in Egypt and was implemented only in the land-reform areas. Demera estate has nine co-operative societies with 4,839 members. Zafaran estate has four societies with 2,142 members, and Maania has one society with 395 members. The control estates have no co-operative societies as such.

Because of the immediate bearing of this co-operative system upon the organization of production, credit, and marketing in the land-reform estates, it is essential to examine its structure and function at some length.

Structure of the co-operative societies. The societies are known as the Egyptian Agricultural Co-operatives of Land Reform. Membership is compulsory for all land-reform beneficiaries. Each member must subscribe to a number of shares equivalent to the number of feddans he acquired—one share per feddan. Membership is permanent as long as the member lives, provided that he continues to be subject to the Agrarian Reform Law. A member may be dismissed from the society if he hinders its work, undermines its status, or fails to fulfill his obligations to it. The Higher Committee for Agrarian Reform has the final decision in this respect. A dismissed member is not entitled to keep the land he acquired; the land taken from him is given to another peasant, who must replace the dismissed member in the co-operative society.

Theoretically, the control and the management of the co-operative societies rest in their elected boards. In practice, however, these responsibilities are taken over by official supervisors from the Higher Committee. The powers of the elected boards are extremely limited: the secretary is responsible only for calling the general meeting twice a year and reporting the minutes; the treasurer is to sign the cash slips along with the official supervisor. The co-operative societies are not entitled to refuse the supervisors appointed by the Higher Committee, to intervene in their duties, or to suspend their powers. The supervisors perform their jobs according to directions specified by the Higher Committee, and they are not entitled to any action breaching these directions.

The members of a society constitute a fairly homogeneous group, since by provision of the Law regarding eligibility for ownership of distributed land, they are all law-abiding Egyptian farmers, over twenty-one years old, who own fewer than five feddans. They all live in the same village and are usually related to each other by blood or by marriages. Their cultural backgrounds, historical circumstances, and physical living conditions are similar. Consequently there is a minimum of social distance among members, and personal interaction is quite frequent. This intimate relationship originated not because of the members' participation in the co-operative society, but because of the village's informal mutual-help arrangements and interfamily relationships. Actually, the participation of the members in the society meetings is extremely limited. General meetings are held only twice a year, and most of the members are not even aware of their membership in the society.

Functions of the co-operative societies. The stated purpose of the co-operative societies is to render all social and agricultural services to the members for the purpose of improving social conditions and increasing farm income. The means for achieving this purpose are dictated by the Higher Committee for Agrarian Reform at Cairo and are executed by official supervisors residing in the localities.

In general, the social services of the co-operative societies do not extend beyond some contributions to charitable and religious objects. For example, all that Demera co-operative society reported as social services in 1956 was a contribution of £E 533 to the mosques in the area, £E 3,000 to the Egyptian Army, and £E 300 worth of clothes to the poor people in the villages. Zafaran co-operative society is constructing 120 new houses to be sold to the members in long term installments. Apart from this housing project, no effort has been made by the co-operative society to improve the social conditions of the farmers in respect to health, education, or recreation.

The most important function of the co-operative societies is to render agricultural services. A major service is the compulsory application of the three-year system of crop rotation. The land-reform estates are divided into large blocks, and each block is further divided into three parts. The peasant who acquired land in a certain block was given a plot in each part. Under the compulsory system of crop rotation, each part must be sown with a single crop and the same crop cannot be cultivated in the same part for two years in succession. This system secures an efficient use of the land without exhausting the soil. It also facilitates the use of machinery, the application of technical agricultural methods, and the performance of farming operations.

Another agricultural service is the provision of necessary farm supplies, such as seeds, fertilizers, agricultural machinery, and cash loans. These supplies are given to each member and charged against him. In 1956, charges for farm supplies on the three surveyed land-reform estates totaled £E 147,179, and there were 7,376 farmer-members of the co-operatives. The average charges were £E 19.95 per member.

The managers of the control estates also provide their tenants with farm supplies, but the quantity is very inadequate. In 1956, charges for farm supplies in the three surveyed control estates totaled £E 28,219, and there were 7,627 tenants. The average charges were £E 3.70 per tenant.

Since the prices per unit of farm supplies and the average size of operating units are exactly the same on the land-reform as on the control estates, it becomes obvious that the co-operative societies provided more than five times the quantity of farm supplies per feddan than did the managers on the control estates. Actually, on the control estates, the tenants are forced to buy farm supplies from the local merchants and to obtain loans from the usurers. In dealing with them, the tenants pay high prices and exorbitant interest rates. Accordingly, the cost of production per feddan becomes higher in the control estates than on the land-reform estates. Average expenses for cultivating one feddan under the three-year system of crop rotation amounted to £E 35.75 on the land-reform estates. The corresponding figure for the control estates was £E 44.54, or 24.6 per cent higher.

Marketing of the members' principal crops is another important agricultural service of the co-operatives. Every member is obliged to sell all his cotton crop and, if necessary, a part of his wheat crop through the society. This co-operative marketing is compulsory for two reasons: (1) to enable each member to achieve a higher price for his crops than if he were to sell individually, and (2) to enable the society to deduct from the sale price the annual installments of the purchase price of the land, government taxes, charges for farm supplies, and the cost of administration.

In case the co-operative societies have a net profit after deducting all liabilities and covering all expenses, 25 per cent of such profit goes into the reserve fund, 20 per cent into the social service fund, and the remaining 55 per cent is divided among the members according to the amount of business each has had with the society during the year. For example, the farmer who delivers ten bales of cotton has contributed twice as much to the business of the co-operative as has the farmer who delivered five bales. If the remaining 55 per cent of the profit amounted to £E 1 per bale, the farmer who delivered ten bales would be entitled to £E 10 and the other farmer to £E 5.

There is no co-operative marketing of field crops in the control estates. All tenants market their crops individually. The managers, in order to insure their collection of rent and other charges, force the tenants to sign a statement that empowers the manager to foreclose the crops sixty days after the harvest if the liabilities are not paid. Guards are assigned by the manager at the expense of the tenants to prevent them from moving the mortgaged crops from the field. The tenants, in order to sell their crops within sixty days must bring the local merchants to the fields to estimate the value of the standing crops. Taking advantage of this situation, the local merchants offer prices well below the market level, and the tenants have no alternative but to accept the price offered.

Improvement of animal production is another agricultural service of the co-operatives on the land-reform estates. Each society has a veterinary center supervised by a veterinarian appointed by the Higher Committee. The center offers medical treatment for sick animals and poultry at reasonable charges. Voluntary livestock insurance is available but not warmly welcomed by the farmers. The insurance covers the healthy cows and water-buffaloes between the ages of three months and fifteen years. Insured livestock receive free medical care and treatment for disease. In case an animal dies because of a specific disease, 75 per cent of its value is paid as compensation to the owner. No compensation is paid for stolen livestock or for death caused by fire, accidents, overwork, neglect, or criminal act. By the end of 1956, this program covered only 12.3 per cent of the livestock liable for insurance on Maania estate and 14.6 per cent on Zafaran estate. The limited participation of the farmers in the program may be attributed to: (1) the unfamiliarity of the peasant with animal insurance and medical treatment (this is actually the first time such a program was implemented in Egypt); (2) the obligations imposed upon the owners of the insured livestock such as recording the milk yield, immunizing the animals against various diseases, and controlling the breeding; (3) the rigid inspection and supervision of the insured livestock by the veterinarian; (4) the limitations imposed upon paying compensation; and (5) the complicated reporting procedure which the farmers must follow in order to collect compensation. All these factors combined discourage the peasant from insuring his livestock.

Another program carried out by the veterinary centers is the distribution of Rhode Island Red chicks, a breed having the advantages of a heavy body and a good yield of big eggs. Each owner is given twelve chicks, one month old, in return for forty-eight fertilized eggs of the yield within one year. The eggs collected from the farmers are incubated and hatched in a hatchery at Cairo. The new chicks are distributed among other farmers in the same manner. The scheme is a continuous procedure working in a cumulative way.

Practically all the new owners in the three land-reform estates are participating in this program. The project is not a success, however, because so many of the distributed chicks die. On Demera estate, 14,388 chicks were distributed at the beginning of 1956, but by the end of that year, only 3,178, or 22.1 per cent, were reported to be surviving. On Itay El-Baroud estate, of which Maania is a part, 26,018 chicks were distributed, and only 3,575, or 13.7 per cent, were reported to be surviving. The high loss of distributed chicks may be attributed to the unsuitability of the village conditions and the farmer's ignorance about the proper care for these chicks. The Higher Committee publishes pamphlets containing instructions for the care of the chicks but they are beyond the comprehension of the vast majority of the farmers, who cannot read.

Other programs for improving livestock production include the distribution of buffalo calves, the establishment of centers for purebred bulls, and the collection and marketing of milk. These projects are still in the initial stages and are being carried out on an experimental basis.

Achievements of the co-operative societies. The organization of the use and cultivation of land, the efficient three-year system of crop rotation, the availability of seeds and fertilizers, and the use of machinery have increased crop production in the land-reform estates.The average yield of cotton per feddan in the three surveyed land-reform estates during 1952-1956 was 13.2 per cent higher than the same average during 1948-1952. The corresponding increase in the control estates was only 2.6 per cent. The average yield of wheat per feddan increased by 21.4 per cent in the land-reform estates and by only 5 per cent in the control estates. The average yield of corn increased by 10.5 per cent in the land-reform estates and by 2.3 per cent in the control estates.

There is no doubt that the land reform co-operative societies have succeeded in their agricultural functions. Production has increased and its cost has decreased. Co-operative marketing has enabled the new owner to receive higher prices for his crops than if he were to sell individually. All these achievements combined have resulted in a considerable increase in the annual net return per feddan. In 1956, the average net return per feddan in the land-reform estates was £E 26.60 as compared to £E 17.70 in 1952—an increase of £E 8.90 per feddan, or 50.3 per cent. The large part of this increase was due to the average annual installment on the purchase price being substantially lower than the average rent paid in 1952. By comparison, the average net return per feddan in the control estates was £E 21.50 in 1956 and £E 17.00 in 1952—an increase of £E 4.50 per feddan, or 26.5 per cent. Practically all this increase is due to the rents being fixed at seven times the basic land tax, considerably lower than rents paid in 1952.

III. Changes in Rural Social Systems

THE RURAL FAMILY

The Egyptian rural family is a closely-knit economic and social group. Family members have a strong sense of belonging to the family group and feel obligated to defend the family honor, to do things for the family, and to be worthy of the family name. These feelings are not limited to the immediate family which consists of the married couple and their children, but it also extends to the joint family and the kinship group. The joint family consists of the paternal grandparents, their unmarried daughters and sons, and their married sons together with their wives and children. The kinship group consists of all those who claim descent from the same paternal ancestor. While the immediate family is relatively limited in its function and significance, the joint family plays an important role in the life of the individual and the community. Its influence is manifested clearly in all social and economic matters, such as marriages, illnesses, funerals, conflicts and feuds, agricultural activities, and mutual aid. The kinship group usually has at its core a main family which patronizes and protects several branch families. Members of the kinship group have traditional obligations toward each other such as assistance in financial difficulties and consultation and aid in all important matters.[5]

Land reform has failed in its intention to create small and independent farm families. Instead of breaking up the traditional network of the joint families and the kinship groups, the reform has strengthened their interaction and widened the scope of their functions. For the purpose of land distribution, the family was defined as "a group of individuals getting their livelihood from one and the same source on the land, no matter whether members of the group reside in one or more places." Before the reform, members of the joint family depended for livelihood on one farm rented by their head. After the reform, land ownership was transferred to this head and the situation did not change. Members of the joint family, no matter whether they reside in one or more places, still depend for livelihood on the land assigned to their head. Moreover, the co-operative societies provided common agricultural functions for the joint families and the kinship groups. Prior to the reform, these family groups farmed their land independently, but after the reform, they were obliged to cultivate the land and market the products co-operatively. This is in contrast to the situation in the control estates where the families are still farming their land and selling their crops independently. Informal mutual-aid arrangements, however, are very frequent among these families and cover most of the agricultural and social activities.

Land reform not only failed in breaking up the structure and composition of the joint families but also failed in introducing significant alterations in their characteristics. In fact, the reform has had a somewhat undesirable effect on marriage and division of labor and no effect on divorce and inheritance.

Marriage. Traditionally, rural families choose the spouses for their children. A go-between is commonly used to conduct the necessary interfamilial negotiations and to conclude the arrangements. In addition to the traditional support for this pattern of marriage, economic and social circumstances act to reinforce the authority of the parents and the acquiescence of the children.

Many factors are considered in the selection of spouses. A basic requirement for an appropriate marriage is that the social and economic status of the two families involved be relatively equal. The more equal their status, the more favorably a marriage is regarded. As a result, kinship marriage is common among rural families. Usually, a male cousin has priority of claim to marry his female cousin, and unless he shows reluctance, she probably cannot marry anybody else.

Some changes have been occurring in this traditional pattern of marriage. Although parental approval continues to be of great importance, forced marriages are not so common. Parents admit that their children are being less obedient about marrying persons whom they do not like. Also the emphasis upon the socio-economic status of the families as a criterion for spouse selection has been somewhat reduced. Personal characteristics of the prospective spouses are being emphasized more and more.

There has been no evidence whatsoever that these changes are taking place as a result of land reform. The pattern of marriage is undergoing the same change in the control estates, and probably in other areas throughout rural Egypt. Land reform, however, has had a direct bearing on the marriage rate. The general trend before reform was toward a slight decline in marriage rate. The rates of 1951 in both the land-reform and control estates and the population census of Egypt indicate this trend. After the Agrarian Reform Law was enacted in 1952, however, the marriage rate increased suddenly on the estates of Demera, Zafaran and Maania after it was announced that these estates would be immediately expropriated and distributed among the inhabitants in holdings from two to five feddans according to the size of the family. Naturally, the farmers wanted to acquire as much land as possible. The only feasible solution was to increase the size of their families by calling home all the members who were working away from the village, and by arranging marriages for the unmarried sons. This resulted in a substantial increase in marriage rates during 1952 and 1953. The rates immediately fell after the land was distributed.

The control estates were exempt from expropriation and distribution, and the marriage rate continued declining through 1952. The trend changed in 1953 after the leases were extended for three years and the rents were fixed below the market level; with the security of tenure and the increase of income, the marriage rate began to increase gradually.

Divorce. A Moslem husband has religious and legal rights to divorce his wife without court procedures, while a Moslem wife can ask for divorce only in the court. Egypt's emancipated women have urged the authorities to consider seriously the enactment of civil legislation that would limit husbands' rights to divorce their wives.

Traditionally, the chief causes of divorce have been the incompatibility of the spouses and the quarrels of the wife with her mother-in-law. There is no evidence that would suggest that land reform has affected the pattern or the rate of divorce. In both the land-reform and control estates, the divorce rates show insignificant changes during the period from 1950 to 1956.

Division of labor. The heavy work on the farm, such as plowing, tilling, and digging and repairing irrigation ditches, is performed by the men of the household. Other work, such as transplanting rice, weeding paddy fields, and picking cotton, is left to women and to children. Usually, the sons help their father and the daughters help their mother. All members of the family work together during the harvest season, especially in transporting and storing the crops. Women too old to work remain at home to take care of the chickens and the babies.

Because the farms are very small, there is usually not enough work available for all the members of large families. This problem is quite serious in the land-reform estates where the co-operative societies are rendering all agricultural services to the members. In the absence of proper means for utilization of leisure, the new owners and their families spend any spare time at their disposal unproductively.

Inheritance. The pattern of passing the family property from one generation to the next is the result of the Islamic laws of inheritance, which prescribe the subdivision of property among all the heirs, each male receiving a portion equal to that of two females. The Agrarian Reform Law included several measures for limiting the subdivision of agricultural land. The Law provided that holdings under five feddans could not be divided through inheritance or by any other means; the heirs must come to an agreement as to the person who shall assume ownership of the land. Because these provisions of the Law have not been enforced, the Islamic laws of inheritance are still observed throughout the country.

THE VILLAGE

Unlike the pattern prevailing in the United States, there are no isolated farmsteads in Egypt. The farmers live in collective villages and go out daily to work in the surrounding fields. The ordinary village consists of a group of mud cottages built close to one another, a mosque for worshipping, and a place for trading and social gatherings. The source of water supply is usually a stream or a spring. In general, the ordinary village lacks most of the facilities considered necessary in a civilized community.

Through its nucleated structure, the village provides its inhabitants with a high degree of personal and group interaction. The influence of the village is strong and effective in situations involving intra-village conflicts, settlement of disputes, moral standards, and social control. This influence also extends to the personal affairs of the inhabitants. The farmer hesitates to take a new step independently or stand against the village's traditions.[6]

Before land reform, village life had been highly feudal, centering around the landlords and their families. The reform, by entirely wiping out rural landlordism, has liberated the peasants and the rural communites from the cruel and rigid control of landlords. With the transfer of land ownership, the peasants achieved a sense of dignity and freedom that created a new life in the villages. With their increased income they also achieved a level of prosperity that could not have been possible otherwise. All this is very obvious in the land-reform villages where the farmers are happy and enthusiastic and show lively appreciation for the change. They now own the village and its land, animals, and machinery. They farm co-operatively and, at least theoretically, have a voice in the complex of agricultural and economic decision making.

The establishment of co-operative societies created a large number of new leaders in the land-reform villages studied. The board members of each society admitted to the writer that they would not be occupying leadership positions had it not been for land reform. At present, the responsibilities of these leaders are very much limited by the control and supervision of the Higher Committee for Agrarian Reform. It is proposed that later the leaders will be left to run the co-operative societies by themselves without interference from above.

The main problem facing the village is the pressure caused by the continuous increase of population on a fixed area of cultivated land. The reform neither solved this problem nor ameliorated its consequences. Birth rates are extremely high and the villages are full of babies born every day. In the land-reform estates, rates of reported births and deaths averaged forty-eight and twenty-one per one thousand population, respectively.

The purpose of the reform was not to extend the cultivated area surrounding the villages but rather to provide for a more equal distribution of the land already cultivated. In doing so, the reform did not solve the problem of increasing population in the rural communities. Moreover, land distribution added to the problem of unemployment. Because there was not enough land for all those who needed it, hundred of families were left without land. Before the reform, most of these families were employed by the landlords as permanent or casual laborers on the estates. As the new owners do not need to employ laborers for their small holdings, some displacement of labor took place. About 8 per cent of the total number gainfully employed on the three land-reform estates in 1952 were unemployed in 1956.

RURAL SOCIAL STRATA

Land expropriation and distribution considerably affected the social stratification inside the land-reform estates. Land expropriation abolished the concentration of wealth in the upper-class landlord families and deprived them of the power and prestige which they had possessed because of their control over the land. The status of the lower-class peasant families changed in a manner which followed exactly the pattern of land distribution. The farmers who acquired land ownership attained thereby a higher social status than that of all other peasants in the estate. Farmers with holdings of from four to five feddans ranked highest, then farmers with from three to four feddans, and then farmers with from two to three feddans. Among those who did not acquire land ownership, peasants with land assigned on a rental basis ranked higher than the rest.

All of these peasant social ranks were within the lower social class. Some of the farm families attained considerably higher social status after the reform, but they did not fill the social gap which existed after the landlord upper-class was abolished. This gap was filled by the official representatives of the Higher Committee for Agrarian Reform. The peasants ranked them above any other group in the estates. They were considered upper-class people because they controlled the distribution, use, and cultivation of land.

The effect of land reform on the rural social strata did not go beyond shifting and reshuffling the peasants within the lower social class, and replacing the landlords with the official representatives. Yet the relationships between the peasants and these officials differ completely from the previous relationships between the peasants and the landlords. The superior-inferior relationship between the landlord and the peasant was based on social, economic, and political exploitation of the peasant by the landlord and was characterized by extreme instability, insecurity, and unrest. The parent-child relationship between the official representative and the peasant is based on emancipating the peasant socially, economically, and politically, and is characterized by stability and security. Yet, the variations in the rights to use and dispose of the land still determine the social status of individuals in the rural communities. The rigid relationship between tenure and social ranking, which existed before the reform, is maintained and probably has become more rigid.

RURAL GOVERNMENTAL AND POLITICAL SYSTEMS

The governmental system. Both the structure and function of the governmental administrative machinery in the villages are very inadequate. The system was established in 1895 and is administered by unpaid officers charged with executing the orders of the central government and maintaining public security in the village. These administrators are the Omdah (mayor) and the Sheikhs who act as his assistants. The Omdah must own ten feddans or more and is elected by certain classes of the villagers. The Sheikhs must also be landowners and are appointed by the government after advisory consultation with village notables. The offices are held for life unless the occupant is dismissed by the central government.

The task of the administrators is to cope with the governmental affairs in the village, such as maintenance of order, collection of government taxes, and military recruitment. As the Omdah is the depository of public authority and the agent of the government in the village, he is equipped with the necessary armed guards that enable him to exercise his powers.

Although the administrative posts are unpaid, the competition for them is very intense. Once a post becomes vacant, especially that of the Omdah, the fight soon begins among the leading families in the village. Whenever a person gets the post, the others make it their job to disturb public security in order to show that the new Omdah is unable to maintain order. They even go so far as to make false accusations against him in order to bring about his dismissal.[7] This intense competition for the administrative posts may be attributed to their attractiveness as positions of great authority with tenure for life.

It is highly surprising that the revolutionary regime, which changed the ruling system and introduced land reform, did not attempt to change or modify this inadequate administrative machinery in the villages. Many reformers in Egypt frequently recommended that this machinery be replaced by a village council elected for a term of not more than five years by all inhabitants of the village. This council should assume the responsibilities of the present administrators along with responsibility for all local affairs pertaining to health, education, public welfare, and village planning.

The political system. The revolutionary government dissolved all the political parties and unified the country under its ideology. Before the reform, political leadership rested in the hands of a small group of landlords. Because of their control over the land, they acquired traditional authority which enabled them to occupy an unchallenged position in political affairs. On the national level, they dominated the two houses of Parliament. On the regional level, they controlled the Province Councils, and on the local level, they dictated to the administrators of the villages.

In electing members of Parliament, peasants have traditionally voted for the political party which their landlord had supported. Consequently, any party which had come into power acted solely for the interests of the landlords, which conflicted with the welfare of the peasants.

The reform, which took away the concentration of wealth in the hands of the landlords, resulted in a tremendous weakening of their political power. Thus opportunities were created for the peasants to participate positively and freely in political decision making. It must be realized, however, that land reform created only the opportunity for democratic political participation in the villages. Whether or not democracy actually will be achieved depends on measures other than land reform.

RURAL EDUCATIONAL SYSTEM

The Ministry of Education administers the school system all over the country. The present system consists of four levels of schools: a six-year primary school, a three-year preparatory school, a three-year secondary school, and a four-year college. Demera is the only one of the surveyed estates that has a preparatory school, while the other estates have only primary schools. Some students go to the neighboring towns and cities to attend schools beyond the levels available in their villages.

In spite of the great effort by the government to improve education throughout the country, the rural educational system has had very disappointing results, due both to the inadequacy of the system itself and to the absence of intellectual stimulus in the rural home.

Inadequacy of the system. The schools on the six surveyed estates are deficient in all respects. Most of the school buildings are overcrowded and lack the necessary facilities for teaching. On Maania estate, for example, the school was housed in an old, mud-brick building with dirty, dark rooms. Three of these rooms were used for administration and storage, and nine rooms served as classrooms for 529 pupils. On Zafaran estate the school building consisted of nine rooms—two rooms had fallen roofs and were not used, two rooms were used for administration, and five rooms were used for classes of 382 pupils. Although all the schools were packed to capacity, they could absorb only one-third of the children at the compulsory age level.

Education in these schools is non-functional, for both the content and the methods reflect earlier patterns of culture, which have been waning for some time. The teachers are unqualified, semi-literate, ill-trained, and nearly isolated from the outside world. They have little conception of the rapid changes that are taking place not only on the national level but on the local level as well. Because of the heavy burden thrown upon their shoulders and the lack of supervision, most of them neglect their pupils and profession. In one of the schools visited, the teacher was responsible for teaching about forty-five children the three R's. The pupils attended the class from 8 A.M. until 2 P.M. Upon the order of their teacher, they opened the book and each pupil in his turn started to read loudly. The teacher then left the room to join other teachers for a gossiping session in the sunny yard of the school. Every now and then he stuck his head in the classroom to make sure discipline was maintained and the pupils were reading.

Absence of intellectual stimulus at home. The environment of the rural household does not stimulate education. The child is overworked and underfed. The parents, being poor and illiterate, prefer to send their children to the fields. They look upon the child as potential earning power and expect him to work and become an economic asset at an early age. Because primary education is compulsory, parents must enroll their children in the school. Between the crop seasons, when there is not much work on the farm, about 95 per cent of those enrolled, encouraged by the free meal offered at noon, usually attend the school. When this meal is cancelled, the attendance drops to 65 per cent. During the crop season when every possible hand is needed to work on the farm, only 30 per cent of the pupils usually attend school.

Most of the houses visited had no facilities that would enable a child to study and to learn. There was no space, light, table, nor chair which a pupil could use for the school homework. The chickens were running from place to place, the buffalo was tied to one corner of the room and the donkey to another. The babies were crying and the grandmother was shouting and threatening. The pupils found it best to leave the house and play outside in the dirt.

Land reform has provided the opportunity for the farmers to send their children to schools. As the co-operative society is organizing the cultivation of the land and rendering all agricultural services, the farmers need not send the children all day to the fields. Yet the reform has not attempted to remedy the disappointing results of the rural educational system by improving conditions in the homes and in the schools. Also, no effort was made to encourage nor to support adult and informal education in the villages. Attendance at the illiteracy campaign classes was steadily decreasing at the time this study was made and informal education was completely lacking in both the land-reform and control estates.

RURAL SOCIAL AGENCIES

Rural health and medical care. Poverty, illiteracy, superstition, bad housing, malnutrition, and shortage of medical facilities and personnel are factors which make health conditions in the Egyptian villages among the worst in the world. As a result of these conditions the peasants have very poor health and low resistance to disease. In both the land-reform and control estates, about 80 per cent of the inhabitants suffer from Bilharziasis, a disease caused by a tiny parasite so agile that it can enter the skin even if there is no fissure. The parasite passes part of its life cycle in the body of a variety of snail which lives in the water of the Nile. Anyone can catch the disease by simple contact with infected water. The farmers, especially those working in the rice fields, are inevitably in contact with such water most of the time.

Free medical treatment is available in both public hospitals and health bureaus. Demera estate has a public hospital operated by one physician and one nurse-aid. It provides medical services to about twenty-four thousand persons. The hospital has forty beds but because its medical budget is limited to £E 60 ($172.00) per month, not more than fifteen beds can be occupied at one time. Moreover, the one physician is unable to meet the community needs for medical treatment. In 1956 a total of 22,780 cases were reported to the clinic for outside treatment. About 60 per cent of these cases were Bilharziasis, 15 per cent were eye diseases, 10 per cent malaria, 10 per cent malnutrition diseases, and 5 per cent other diseases. During that year 1,407 babies were brought to the clinic: 22 per cent of these children had epidemic diseases; 20 per cent, skin diseases; 18 per cent, eye diseases; 15 per cent, lung diseases; and 25 per cent, other diseases. No deliveries had been performed in the hospital since it was established in November, 1955.

Maania estate's public hospital operates in much the same way as does the hospital on Demera estate. Zafaran estate has only a health bureau, which provides first-aid treatment and vaccination against epidemic diseases. The nearest public hospital, nine miles away in Beyala, is serving the inhabitants of both Beyala Wakf estate and Zafaran land-reform estate.

All these medical institutions are administered by the Ministry of Public Health and are not connected with the Higher Committee for Agrarian Reform.

Rural social welfare service. In 1941 the Ministry of Social Affairs introduced a scheme for establishing social welfare centers in the villages. Each center was designed to serve about ten thousand people and was to consist of a meeting hall, a dispensary, a maternity home, a pure water system, a workshop for small handicrafts, and a rural club. The scheme progressed very slowly and in 1953 there were only 180 centers serving 12 per cent of the rural population.

In 1954, the Higher Council for Public Services introduced another scheme for establishing collective units consisting of a school, a hospital, and a social welfare center. The Council requested £E 4,600,000 for establishing two hundred of these units in the villages.

At the end of 1956 the land-reform and control estates had neither social welfare centers nor collective units. Demera estate had a welfare center before land reform, but it has been closed since 1952.

Rural extension service. The task of extension work is: (a) to extend to the farm families the findings of science that can be applied to their farming, homemaking, and other aspects of living; and (b) to present the farmers' problems to research specialists for study and analysis. The guiding principle to be followed in performing this task is to work with the people rather than for the people. The aim is to solve or ameliorate the problems which the people recognize as important, and to help them recognize solutions for problems which they have accepted as inevitable.[8]

The extension service system of land reform deals only with agricultural problems. Its programs are directed from the top down and are carried out for the farmers rather than with the farmers. Obligatory supervised co-operative societies were established for the new owners in the land-reform estates to implement these programs. On the small holding assigned to the peasant, technical agricultural methods are applied, modern machinery and selected seeds and chemical fertilizers are used, efficient systems of crop rotation are followed, and field products are sold co-operatively. These scientific modern techniques were adopted by the co-operative societies to replace the primitive traditional farming operations of the peasants. The new methods were introduced not because the peasant himself recognized or was helped to recognize the inefficiency of the old practices, but simply because this inefficiency was recognized by the Higher Committee for Agrarian Reform. In the meantime, this committee made no effort to help the peasants solve many of the problems which the peasants themselves recognize as important. The inhabitants of Zafaran village, for example, are very much aware of the inadequacy of the fallen school building and the scarcity of medical facilities in the health bureau, yet, the Higher Committee has ignored these problems.

The Higher Committee presents to research specialists for study and analysis only those farmers' problems related to technical improvement of agricultural and animal production. The faculty staff of the College of Agriculture at Alexandria University and the specialists of the Egyptian Agricultural Organization are conducting several experiments in the land-reform estates on intensive cultivation, diversification of farming, and improvement of livestock. In the meantime, technical improvement of education, health, recreation, and other social conditions are not being considered by land-reform officials.

CHAPTER V

The Effect of Land Reform on Rural Families

THE purpose of the preceding chapter was to evaluate the effect of land reform on rural communities with emphasis on the agrarian structure and the structure of rural social systems. The purpose of the present chapter is to analyze the effect of land reform on rural families with emphasis on the socio-economic levels and the attitudes of the farmers. For this purpose, intensive interviews were conducted with six hundred family heads from the surveyed land-reform and control estates. The interviewees consisted of two equal-size groups. The family heads in the first group were selected from the surveyed land-reform estates by stratified random sampling. They were tenant-cultivators who acquired ownership of the land in 1953 when the Agrarian Reform Law was enacted. The family heads in the second group were tenant-cultivators from the control estates who did not acquire ownership of the land. They were selected to match the family heads in the first group with respect to age, sex, education, size of farm, size of family, and area of location. The fundamental rule observed in matching the family heads was to vary the land-reform factor and to maintain constant other factors which tend to influence the socio-economic level and attitudes of the farmers. In this sense, the second group served as a control device.[1]

It must be emphasized that the family heads in the two groups were not selected to represent a cross section of the farm population throughout Egypt. They were selected only to represent a specialized group, and the results of their interviews should be interpreted as such.

The interviews attempted to elicit information about the changes effected in socio-economic conditions and in the attitudes of farmers during the period from 1952 to 1956. It was hypothesized that the family heads in the two groups were drawn from the same parent population and that, therefore, any observed difference between the groups is of a magnitude that occurs very frequently as a fluctuation of random sampling.

In order to test this hypothesis, the data obtained from the interviewees were processed for statistical analysis, and the results were correlated with four independent variables: (a) age, (b) education, (c) size of farm, and (d) size of family. Statistically, the stated hypothesis implies that the coefficient of correlation between the distribution patterns of the two groups is perfect ($r=1.0$). The hypothesis must be rejected if the true value of the difference between the observed and hypothetical coefficients is significantly different from zero. Accordingly, the t value for the standard error of this difference was computed and interpreted at the 1 per cent level of significance. The emphasis in the interpretation was placed on the differences between the coefficients of correlation rather than on the magnitude of these coefficients.[2]

I. General Characteristics of the Interviewees

The group of land-reform owners in the sample was drawn from the expropriated estates of Demera, Zafaran, and Maania, which were distributed in 1953. Each of these estates is represented by one hundred farm families. The control group of non-land-reform tenant-cultivators was selected from the estates of Shawa, Beyala, and Saft-Khaled, which were exempt from expropriation and distribution. Each of these estates is also represented by one hundred farm families.

AGE AND SEX COMPOSITION

The land-reform owners in the sample were male family heads between the ages of twenty-five and sixty-five. About 12 per cent were under thirty, 68 per cent were between thirty and fifty, and 20 per cent were over fifty. The average age was 41.6 years. The control group was selected to match the land-reform group in respect to age and sex.

EDUCATIONAL COMPOSITION

Exactly 86 per cent of the land-reform owners in the sample were illiterate. They had no education and were completely unable to read and write. Another 3 per cent attended illiteracy campaign classes and could hardly write their names. About 9 per cent attended El-Kottab, a one-room private school where children are taught to memorize the Koran by rote. Although these men had memorized parts of the Koran, their reading and writing were very poor. Only 2 per cent of the owners attended elementary and above elementary-level schools, and are actually the only farmers that could be considered educated.

The control group was selected to match the land-reform group in respect to education.

SIZE OF FARM

The size of the farms studied varied from two to five feddans. About 49 per cent of the land-reform owners acquired two to three feddans, 35 per cent acquired from over three to four feddans, and 16 per cent acquired from over four to five feddans. The average size of the farms was 3.2 feddans. The control group was matched with the land-reform group in respect to size of farms.

SIZE OF FAMILY

While some families consisted only of a married couple and their unmarried children, other families consisted of married couples, their unmarried sons and daughters, and their married sons along with their wives and children. The size of families varied considerably, the average number of members being 6.6. In the land-reform group, 8 per cent of the families had two to four members, 72 per cent had five to seven members, 17 per cent had eight to ten members, and 3 per cent had more than ten members. The control group was selected to match the land-reform group in respect to size of families.

II. Changes in Economic Conditions

FARM INCOME

In 1956, families in the land-reform group had an average net farm income for the year of £E 96.30, 20 per cent higher than the corresponding figure of £E 80.20 for the control group. The income difference between land-reform and control-group families with larger farms was greater than it was between the families in the two groups with smaller farms. The average difference was £E 12 between families in the two groups with two feddans, and £E 29 between families in the two groups with four feddans. Because the land-reform estates were distributed according to the ages and number of family members, the average income difference was also greater between larger land-reform and control-group families than it was between smaller families in the two groups. Thus, while the average difference was £E 6 between families in the two groups with four members, it was £E 21 between families in the two groups with ten members. Interpretation of *t* values indicated a highly significant difference between the family heads in the two groups with respect to farm income.

The considerable increase in farm income of the land-reform group may be attributed to these factors: (a) the annual installments paid by the land-reform group were substantially less than the rents paid by the control group; (b) the productivity of the land-reform farms was slightly higher than the productivity of the control farms because of the heavier use of fertilizers and seeds, deeper plowing by tractors, and better use and cultivation of land; and (c) co-operative marketing of crops was highly organized among the farmers in the land-reform group, while in the control group, farmers were individually selling their farm crops to the local merchants.

VALUE OF LIVESTOCK AND POULTRY

The average value of livestock and poultry owned by families in the land-reform was £E 123.40, slightly less than the corresponding figure of £E 123.70 for the control group. Interpretation of *t* values showed no significant difference between the two groups in this respect, which may be attributed to: (a) the ineffectiveness of land-reform programs for distributing buffalo calves and Rhode Island Red chicks; and (b) the failure of the program for improving animal production to induce the land-reform owners to keep more livestock and poultry.

FAMILY EXPENSES

Data were obtained about family spending in 1956 for certain items: meat, clothing, tea, coffee, sugar, cigarettes, and tobacco These items along with family spending for traditional celebrations were selected because they make up a major part of the expenditures of the rural family.

In 1956, families in the land-reform group spent an average of

£E 11 for meat, which represented 11.4 per cent of the average family net income. The corresponding figure of £E 10.20 for the control group was 7.3 per cent lower and represented 12.7 per cent of the average family net income. Interpretation of *t* values indicated, however, that the only significant difference in spending occurred between the large families in the land-reform group and in the control group. This may be attributed to the fact that the income difference between the large families in the land-reform and in the control group was considerably higher than the corresponding difference between the small families in the two groups.

Families in the land-reform group spent an average of £E 20.90 for clothing in 1956, which represented 21.7 per cent of the average family net income. The corresponding figure of £E 20.30 for the control group was 2.9 per cent lower and represented 25.3 per cent of the average family net income. Interpretation of *t* values showed no significant difference between the spending of the two groups. The land-reform families failed to devote any considerable proportion of their increased income for better or more clothing.

Spending for tea, coffee, sugar, tobacco, and cigarettes averaged £E 21.90 in 1956 for land-reform families, and represented 22.7 per cent of the average family net income. The corresponding figure of £E 17.70 for the control group was 19.2 per cent lower and represented 22.1 per cent of the average family net income. Interpretation of *t* values indicated a highly significant difference between the families in the two groups. The land-reform families were spending a considerable proportion of their increased income for tea, coffee, sugar, tobacco, and cigarettes, and thus bought and consumed more of these items than did the families in the control group.

Family spending for traditional celebrations averaged £E 14.40 in 1956 for the land-reform group, which represented 15 per cent of the average family net income. The corresponding figure of £E 11.70 for the control group was 18.8 per cent lower, and represented 14.6 per cent of the average family net income. Interpretation of *t* values showed a significant difference between the land-reform group and the control group in respect to family spending for traditional celebrations.

It can be concluded that land reform, by increasing the income of the new owners, has increased their purchasing. The new owners bought more meat, tea, coffee, sugar, cigarettes, and tobacco, and they also spent more than the control group on traditional celebrations.

METHOD OF PAYMENT FOR ITEMS PURCHASED

In the land-reform group, 19 per cent of the families paid cash for the items purchased in 1956 while 81 per cent bought these items on credit. In the control group, 6 per cent paid for the purchased items in cash while 94 per cent bought these items on credit. Interpretation of t values showed no significant difference between the methods of payment by the family heads in the two groups.

Land reform, although significantly increasing the income and thus the purchasing power of the farmers, did not induce them to pay in cash for the items purchased. Their continued use of credit may be attributed to the distribution of dividends by the co-operative societies only once a year, which means that ready cash is not available to the farmers.

DEBT CONDITION

In the land-reform group, 31 per cent were in debt in both 1952 and 1956. About 3 per cent were in debt only in 1956, 31 per cent were in debt only in 1952, and 35 per cent were neither in debt in 1952 nor in 1956. In the control group, 40 per cent were in debt in both 1952 and 1956, 3 per cent were in debt only in 1956, 19 per cent were in debt only in 1952, and 38 per cent were neither in debt in 1952 nor in 1956. Interpretation of t values indicated no significant difference between the two groups. Land reform failed to induce the new owners to improve their debt condition in spite of the increase in their income.

III. Changes in Social Conditions

MUTUAL-HELP ARRANGEMENTS

In 1956 all the family heads in the land-reform group and in the control group were helped on the farm by unpaid family members. About 72 per cent of the land-reform group and all of the control group received additional unpaid help from neighbors and relatives other than family members. Interpretation of t values indicated no significant difference between the two groups.

Land reform, although intended to create small independent

farmers, had no significant effect on the prevailing family and kinship mutual-help network. The 28 per cent of the land-reform group who did not receive unpaid help from relatives and neighbors may not have needed it, due to the many agricultural services performed for them by the co-operatives.

HEALTH AND MEDICAL CARE

In the land-reform group, 45 per cent of the family heads mentioned public hospitals as a place of treatment; 24 per cent mentioned non-professional practitioners; 6 per cent, barber shops; and 25 per cent, inquiring about folk remedies from neighbors.

In the control group, 45 per cent of the family heads mentioned public hospitals; 23 per cent mentioned non-professional practitioners; 7 per cent, barber shops; and 25 per cent, inquiring about folk remedies from neighbors.

Concerning attitudes toward public hospitals, 24 per cent of the family heads in the land-reform group mentioned that they have no particular feelings toward public hospitals, 60 per cent mentioned that they have a feeling of security toward public hospitals, 5 per cent mentioned that there is no proper care at public hospitals, and 11 per cent mentioned that they are suspicious of public hospitals.

In the control group, 33 per cent of the family heads mentioned that they have no particular feelings toward public hospitals, 55 per cent mentioned that they have a feeling of security toward public hospitals, and 12 per cent mentioned that they are suspicious of hospitals.

Interpretation of t values indicated no significant difference between the two groups in respect to place of treatment for illness and attitudes toward public hospitals. It is obvious that land reform did not induce the new owners to seek better treatment for illness in spite of the increase in their income.

EDUCATION AND COMMUNICATION MEDIA

Number of children in school. In the land-reform group, 56 per cent of the families had no children in school, 40 per cent had one child in school, and 4 per cent had two children in school. In the control group, 65 per cent had no children in school, 33 per cent had one child in school, and 2 per cent had two children in school. Interpretation of t values indicated no significant difference between the two groups. Land reform failed to create an intellectual stimulus that would motivate the new owners to send their children to schools instead of to the fields.

Availability of radio sets. In the land-reform group, 4 per cent owned radio sets and listened to the radio, 29 per cent did not own radio sets but listened to radio in coffee shops or other places, and 67 per cent neither owned radio sets nor listened to radio. In the control group, 2 per cent owned radio sets and listened to radio, 19 per cent did not own radio sets but listened to radio in coffee shops, and 79 per cent neither owned radio sets nor listened to radio.

In the land-reform group, 15 per cent of those who listened to radio indicated preference for Koran; 13 per cent preferred news; 31 per cent, songs; 10 per cent, stories; and 31 per cent, rural programs. In the control group, 12 per cent of those who listened to radio indicated preference for Koran; 11 per cent preferred news; 33 per cent, songs; 20 per cent, stories; and 24 per cent, rural programs.

Interpretation of t values indicated no significant difference between the two groups in respect to the number of families who owned radio sets, the number of those who listened to radio, and the kinds of programs they preferred. It must be noted, however, that more of the land-reform group preferred rural programs, while more of the control group preferred stories. News programs attracted the attention of the farmers in 1956 because of the peculiar circumstances resulting from the Anglo-French-Israeli attack on the Suez Canal.

HOUSING CONDITIONS

The room-person ratio was 0.44 for the land-reform group, and 0.45 for the control group. None of the members of the land-reform group or the control group had running water in their homes.

Since 1952 about 83 per cent of the land-reform group and 88 per cent of the control group have made no changes in their homes. Among those in the land-reform group who made some changes in their homes, 43 per cent mentioned painting, 29 per cent mentioned repairing, and 28 per cent mentioned the addition of rooms. Among those in the control group who made some changes in their homes, 60 per cent mentioned painting, 15 per cent mentioned repairing, and 25 per cent mentioned the addition of rooms.

Interpretation of t values indicated no significant difference between the land-reform and the control group in respect to number of rooms in the house, room-person ratio, running water, and changes that have taken place in the house since 1952. It can be concluded, therefore, that land reform did not induce the farmers to improve their housing conditions.

RECREATION AND UTILIZATION OF LEISURE

In the land-reform group, 14 per cent of the family heads mentioned that they spent leisure time at their own homes; 20 per cent mentioned neighbors' homes; 18 per cent, coffee shops; 6 per cent, mosques; 30 per cent, gathering places; and 12 per cent, simply idling. In the control group, 20 per cent of the family heads mentioned that they spent leisure time at their own homes; 24 per cent mentioned neighbors' homes; 8 per cent, coffee shops; 8 per cent, mosques; 27 per cent gathering places; and 13 per cent, idling.

Interpretation of t values indicated a significant difference between the two groups. The land-reform owners were spending a considerable part of their leisure time in coffee shops and other gathering places, which may be attributed both to the significant increase in their income and the absence of adequate measures for utilization of leisure.

There was no significant difference, however, between the two groups in respect to the recreational activities which their members preferred. Of the land-reform group, 14 per cent preferred outdoor and indoor games; 49 per cent preferred informal gatherings; 37 per cent, celebrations. Of the control group 13 per cent preferred outdoor and indoor games; 49 per cent preferred informal gatherings; and 38 per cent, celebrations.

ORGANIZATIONAL PARTICIPATION

There were no organizations established for or by the control group, but all members of the land-reform group belonged to the co-operative societies established by the Higher Committee for Agrarian Reform. Only 9 per cent of the family heads in this group, however, were aware of their membership in these societies. The others failed to realize either that they were members or that the services which they received were rendered by co-operative societies. The only members of the co-operatives they mentioned were their representatives on the boards, and they indicated that "land-reform" rendered all the services. Yet, most of the farmers appeared to have complete confidence in their representatives, although they were not totally satisfied with the services rendered. They indicated the need for housing projects, recreational facilities, medical care, and industrialization programs.

In the absence of any organizations established for the control group, no comparison could be made for organizational participation. The data presented, however, indicate clearly the lack of active participation in the land-reform co-operative organizations, the lack of awareness which the new owners had of their membership in these societies, and the need for social services.

IV. Changes in Attitudes

ATTITUDES TOWARD FAMILY LIFE

During interviews family heads responded to questions concerning their attitudes toward certain aspects of family life such as marriage, divorce, size of family, birth control, and freedom of children to choose their prospective spouses. Interpretation of t values indicated no significant difference between the two groups in respect to attitudes as correlated with age, education, size of family, and size of farm.

About 64 per cent of the land-reform group and 73 per cent of the control group preferred early marriages. They indicated that because their life span is short, early marriages would enable them to establish a family and leave behind grown children. On the other hand, 36 per cent of the land-reform group and 27 per cent of the control group preferred late marriages. They indicated that marriage should be postponed until a man is physically and economically able to establish and support a family.

Only 2 per cent of the land-reform group and 3 per cent of the control group were in favor of obliging the husbands to go to court in case of divorce. On the other hand, 98 per cent of the land-reform group and 97 per cent of the control group opposed divorce through court and maintained that it is the man's religious and legal right to divorce his wife without court procedures.

In the land-reform group, 63 per cent preferred large families and 37 per cent preferred small families. About 11 per cent preferred the children to be all boys, 61 per cent preferred the children to be mostly boys, 23 per cent preferred the children to be boys as well as girls, and 5 per cent indicated that sex makes no difference. About 73 per cent were in favor of giving boys a status superior to that of girls.

In the control group, 73 per cent preferred large families and 27 per cent preferred small families. About 14 per cent preferred the children to be all boys, 66 per cent preferred the children to be mostly boys, 16 per cent preferred the children to be boys as well as girls, and 4 per cent indicated that sex of children makes no difference. About 81 per cent were in favor of giving boys a superior status.

Concerning attitudes toward birth control, 10 per cent of the land-reform group were in favor of birth control, 7 per cent were against it, and 83 per cent had never heard of it. In the control group, 9 per cent were in favor of birth control, 4 per cent were against it, and 87 per cent had never heard of it.

As to the attitudes toward allowing children to choose their prospective spouses, 43 per cent of the land-reform group were in favor of allowing the son to choose his wife, and only 2 per cent were in favor of allowing the daughter to choose her husband. In the control group, 37 per cent were in favor of allowing the son to choose his wife, and 3 per cent were in favor of allowing the daughter to choose her husband. About 36 per cent of the land-reform group and 25 per cent of the control group were in favor of educating girls. Yet, only 17 per cent of the land-reform group, and 14 per cent of the control group would allow their daughters to work or live away from home.

Since the t values have indicated no significant difference between the two groups in respect to all of these attitudes, it can be concluded that land reform had no effect on the rigid conformity of the farmers to rural Egypt's deep-rooted customs and traditions. This result was expected because land reform has strengthened the social control of the village and the rural family. It must be realized, too, that no real change in attitudes could occur during the short period which has elapsed since the introduction of land reform.

ATTITUDES TOWARD LAND REFORM

Land-reform critics in Egypt expressed some doubt concerning the attitudes of the new owners toward the reform. In 1956, it was found that most of these owners were satisfied with the land-reform program. About 89 per cent of the owners in the sample indicated that land reform had been beneficial to their villages and to their families. They mentioned that without land reform, living conditions would have been worse than they are at present. Only 11 per cent indicated that their villages and their families had not benefited from land reform. They mentioned that without land reform, living conditions would have been better than they are at present.

The farmers' evaluation of the land-reform program seems to be based upon the actual benefits they themselves have derived from the distribution of land. Those who mentioned that the reform had not benefited their villages and their families were not satisfied with the distribution procedure and indicated that the land assigned to them was not enough for family needs. All the farmers in the land-reform group, however, were pleased to own the land which they cultivate and indicated that they have no desire whatsoever to be tenants again.

CHAPTER VI

An Outlook for Social Development

THE Agrarian Reform Law was regarded as one of the greatest achievements of the new regime in Egypt. Although the Law was enacted under a revolutionary government, its provisions were quite moderate. Landowners were allowed to retain two hundred feddans for themselves and an additional one hundred feddans for their children. Under Egyptian conditions, this represents an annual income of at least £E 6,000. Furthermore, the Law provided compensation for expropriated owners and encouraged them to invest their savings in land reclamation, mining, and industry.

In the preceding chapters, the provisions of the Law were discussed and their effects on rural communities and farm families were analyzed. This chapter provides a comprehensive critique of the Law, considers the possible prospects of the changes effected, and recommends further measures to foster social development.

I. A Critique of the Agrarian Reform Law

NECESSITY OF THE LAW

The main argument for the enactment of the Agrarian Reform Law was the need for securing a more equal distribution of land and income by abolishing the strong concentration of landed wealth, eliminating institutional monopoly in land tenure, and distributing large estates among the landless peasants. This need represented certain nationalistic goals of the revolutionary government that took precedence over property rights, but these goals also corresponded with the private interests of the individual peasants who demanded land. In fact, the chief pressure for reform legislation came from these peasants, though until the revolutionary government came into power, there was no channel through which they could express their interests or satisfy their needs.

The few who argued against the enactment of the Law referred to countries which advanced without drastic land-reform measures, comparing their economic, social, or political situation with that of Egypt. One argument maintained that instead of transferring land ownership to the tenants, the government could have enacted legislation for regulating the landlord-tenant relationship. Those supporting the argument referred to England, where tenancy is successfully regulated by laws. They overlooked the fact that land in England is only one of the many forms of holding wealth. If the British landlord attempts to charge exorbitant rents, the tenant can invest his capital in other ways.[1] In Egypt, because of the limited industrial and commercial activities, landless peasants are forced to rely on agriculture for their living, working either as tenants or laborers.

A second argument maintained that there was no need for expropriating land from large landowners. Instead, in order to provide for a more equal distribution of land ownership, landless peasants could be given special credit facilities for purchasing land. Those supporting this argument referred to Switzerland, Denmark, and Sweden where the land system has gradually adjusted itself without drastic changes. But how could the tenure system in Egypt adjust itself when ownership was concentrated in a small minority who regarded their land as a source of social prestige and political power? There was no price which the peasants could pay that the landlords would be willing to accept.[2]

A third argument suggested that progressive taxation would be an adequate remedy for the tenure system. Again, however, progressive taxation would not have been effective in a country like Egypt where landlords had occupied an unchallenged position of dominance. The landlords would have escaped such taxes, either directly by using their influence, or indirectly by increasing the rental values of their land.[3]

A fourth argument claimed that the division of large estates would cause a decline in land productivity. This argument had no validity for several reasons. First, the large estates in most cases were already divided and leased to small tenants and were not actually large producing units. The transfer of land ownership to the operating tenants could not affect the scale of operation and production or the size of operating units. Secondly, the Law provided for the establishment of co-operative societies to organize the use and cultivation of land and to render all agricultural services to the new owners, which meant that the distributed estates were to be operated as large enterprises. Thirdly, it was not the primary purpose of the Law to secure an over-all increase in agricultural production, but rather to provide a more equal distribution of income and property of land: even if land distribution would have resulted in a decrease of the total productivity, the purpose of the Law would not have been defeated. This does not mean, however, that the effectiveness of land reform as a means of increasing agricultural production should not be considered.[4]

SCOPE OF THE LAW

The scope of the Agrarian Reform Law was rather limited. Expropriation measures affected only about 11 per cent of the total cultivated area, belonging to 1,789 landowners. Of the total expropriated land, about one-third was the property of the former Royal family. Most of the remainder was held by some twenty families who had occupied a powerful political position in the country.

The land actually available for distribution was less than the area liable to expropriation, and amounted to only 6 per cent of the total cultivated area.[5] The number of those who acquired ownership of land is estimated to be 145,000, or about 3.5 per cent of the total gainfully employed in agriculture.[6]

The regulation of the landlord-tenant relationship benefited far more people than did the distribution of land, for four million tenants continued to rent an area of 3,600,000 feddans, or 60.7 per cent of the total cultivated land.

Judging the Law by its limited scope, there are those who claim that the reform is useless because it could not provide enough land to give farms of adequate size to all the landless families. It is true that the reform did not provide land for all who need land, not, however, because of deficiencies in the Law, but rather because the demand for reform did not become acute until the cultivated area was by no means adequate to support the people on the land. The fact that everyone cannot receive land does not prove that no one should be given land.[7] What it does prove is the need for further measures to improve the conditions of those who are still without land.

DEFICIENCIES IN THE DESIGN OF THE LAW

As stated earlier, the Agrarian Reform Law provided for several organized governmental actions, which include: expropriation and redistribution of agricultural land in excess of a maximum limit, establishment of co-operative organizations for the new owners, prevention of undue subdivision and fragmentation of agricultural land, regulation of the landlord-tenant relationship, and provisions for improving the condition of farm laborers. Each of these provisions had certain inherent deficiencies which require special evaluation.

Limitation of individual ownership. In limiting the individual ownership of land to two hundred feddans throughout the country, no consideration was given to local variations in land productivity, nor to the variations in the amount of land owned over the maximum limit. Thus, no distinction was made between two hundred feddans of productive land and the same area of poor land, nor between an owner with four hundred feddans and another with four thousand feddans.

Different approaches to the limitation of land ownership have been made in various countries. In Italy the Stialcio Law made the percentage of land requisitioned in inverse proportion to its fertility. In Finland the extent of the land requisitioned was in proportion to the size of holding. Egypt's approach of limiting land ownership to two hundred feddans throughout the country, however, had its administrative merits in facilitating requisition procedures.

Land rent and land prices. The Agrarian Reform Law fixed land rent at seven times the basic land tax and land prices at ten times the rent or seventy times the land tax.

Land taxes had been based on an assessment of rental values for divisions of land which were similar in irrigation facilities, drainage, distance from market, soil composition, and other physical conditions. The latest rental estimates were made in 1946, and the tax was set up at 14 per cent of the estimated rental value.

The rental values established in 1946, although representing economic conditions peculiar to that year, were considered in 1952 as a basis for compensation and purchase rates. As a result, landowners were compensated at rates much below the market value of their land. Landlords who had used their influence in the past to secure a low tax assessment were "hoist with their own petard." Peasants who acquired land on fully assessed estates paid relatively more than those who acquired land on under-assessed estates.[8] All of these peasants, however, paid prices well below the market value.

Ghonemy believes that by fixing rental values at seven times the basic land tax, land rent will be inflexible. He stated that a frozen demand and supply price of the use of land will exist year after year regardless of variations in output and prices of products.[9] Ghonemy, in making such a statement, has overlooked the fact that the cultivated area in Egypt is extremely limited, and the demand for land is steadily rising. Under these conditions, a continuous enforcement of a fixed rent is rather impossible. In fact, there is already available evidence to prove that agricultural land in some areas is leased in contravention of the Law. In 1953, the Ministry of Wakf leased the land of Beyala estate, in accordance with the Law, at seven times the basic land tax. The following year, after discovering that rents in some parts of the estate were much below the market level, the Ministry found a clever way to escape the provisions of the Law. The productive land with a low tax assessment was leased on a share-cropping basis, and the tenants were obliged to buy the share of the Ministry for a definite price fixed at £E 8.19. This price, which the tenant paid for the use of the land, amounted to sixteen times the land tax and exceeded the legal rent by over 100 per cent in some parts of the estate. Thus a governmental agency evaded the Law only one year after it was enacted. Further evidence proves that some landowners, encouraged by their right to set aside the occupancy of tenants in half of the area rented, were selling new rent contracts to these peasants. These leases were contracted in writing at seven times the basic land tax, but before the owner signed, the peasants had to pay in advance the difference between the market and the legal levels for rent. Some landowners went as far as to issue the leases to those who offered the highest prices.

Land distribution. The requisitioned land was distributed among small farmers in holdings of from two to five feddans. The underlying principle of land distribution was to provide the farmer and his family with an income exceeding by 10 per cent the cost of their bare necessities. The size of the holding assigned to a land-reform owner was determined on the basis of the productive capacity per feddan, the average cost of living, the size of the family, and the ages of family members.

All these variables do change with time. The land that was productive in 1952 will be more or less productive ten years later. The cost of living and the size of the family will increase or decrease, and the age composition of the family will change. Consequently, the land which provided the farmer and his family with an income sufficient to meet their basic needs in 1952 may or may not be adequate ten years later.

From the new owners' point of view, this constitutes a serious problem. Before land reform, they were tenant cultivators renting plots of land which varied in size; each peasant used to rent the area he and his family could cultivate, and to adjust the size of this area whenever needed. After the reform, the peasant and his family became limited to the area assigned to them by the Law, for he is not free to sell, sublet, farm independently, or adjust the size of his farm.

Co-operative organizations. The Law obliged the farmers who acquired ownership of land to join co-operative organizations supervised by the Higher Committee for Agrarian Reform. These organizations have the power to render all agricultural and social services in behalf of their members.

As a basic principle, a co-operative organization must possess three distinctive characteristics: (a) The association should spring from a felt need and membership must be voluntary; (b) the decisions must be arrived at democratically and should not be dictated by external authorities; and (c) the profits must be distributed in proportion to the use which each member makes of the organization.

The organizations established for the land-reform owners—being obligatory, supervised, and imposed from above—cease to be co-operative because they lack the first two characteristics of co-operation. They do possess, however, the third characteristic because the dividends from the profits are distributed among the members according to the transactions of each with the organization. This attribute by itself is highly significant because it distinguishes the so-called co-operative organizations of land reform from the collective enterprises. As stated by Menon:

> There is one important distinction between a co-operative and collective organization which has to be kept in mind:

> in the co-operative, whatever form it might take, ownership rights are definitely recognized and paid for, either in the shape of rent or dividend or some participation in profits; in the collective, ownership rights are forfeited either to the state or to the collective unit and do not carry any claim to a share of the proceeds.[10]

The same distinction also was made by Schiller. He stated that:

> The co-operative is an association of free and autonomous economic units, whereas the collective enterprise consists of members who have lost their economic autonomy.[11]

There is no doubt that the organizations established for the new land-reform owners are not collective enterprises. Whether or not these organizations are of a co-operative nature involves several questions. Sir Malcolm Darling described these organizations as "based upon wedding the co-operative method to the paternal with the new owner as their child." But he wonders whether a co-operative society which requires that all concerned people must join can prove "as fully co-operative in fact as in name." He stated that "co-operation will never take firm root in agricultural soil without a proper understanding of its principles." Therefore, he believes that a strong educational effort could create a co-operative spirit for which the Egyptian village is good ground.[12] Warriner stated that:

> There are some real co-operative societies in existence, as, for example, the star example of Zafaran; but the newly created ones are artificial.[13]

Subdivision of holdings. The Law stipulated, as a solution for the problem of fragmentation, that holdings under five feddans should not be divided whether through sale, exchange, inheritance, or any other means. The parties concerned must come to an agreement as to the persons who shall assume ownership of the land.

These measures have not been executed in practice, and probably will never be, for several reasons. First, because the personal feeling of the peasant for his soil is very strong, agreement of the parties concerned to give up their shares in land is nearly impossible. Second, because agricultural land still maintains its value as a source of social prestige, agreement of the parties concerned as to who should assume ownership of the land is very difficult. Third, the transfer of all shares in land to one owner will deprive the rest of the parties concerned of a stable source of income. Even if they get an adequate compensation for their shares, they will lack the experience to invest it in a commercial or an industrial enterprise. Fourth, these measures, if they are to succeed, must overcome the sacred inheritance laws of Islam, which the people have accepted unquestioningly. Fifth, these measures offer only a solution limiting future subdivision of the land without tackling the existing problem of fragmented holdings.

Actually, the success of any enacted measures for solving the problem of fragmentation will be impossible for many years. Such measures must be postponed until the socio-economic well-being and the sense of civic participation of landowners have had several years of development. At present, a solution imposed from above will create nothing but complete dissatisfaction among farm people.

Wages of agricultural labor. The Law provided that the wages of agricultural workers should be fixed annually by an official committee appointed by the Minister of Agriculture. In a subsequent decree the Minister of Agriculture laid down minimum wage rates throughout the country at £E 0.18 per day for fully grown men, and £E 0.10 for women, boys, and girls.

These rates did not take into consideration the differences in labor demand and supply in various agricultural districts. In many areas, they were considered high for the prevailing local conditions. Moreover, these rates do not apply to agricultural laborers employed by the authorities concerned to perform duties in the public interest. Consequently, the minimum rates have not generally been enforceable.

DEFICIENCIES IN THE LAND-REFORM POLICY

Land reform must be considered a continuous process which should not be ended by the changes of tenure arrangements or the distribution of land. This principle has been realized by the Higher Committee for Agrarian Reform in Egypt. What this Committee has not realized is that "it is simply not the land but the man on the land that creates problems."[14]

Following land distribution the Committee devoted its time and effort to increase land productivity and improve livestock. But no direct effort has been made to improve the social conditions of the new owner. The farmer's livestock, for example, received more consideration from the Committee than the farmer himself or his family. Thus: (a) while a veterinarian was appointed for the treatment of livestock, no physician was appointed for the treatment of the farmer and his family; (b) life and medical insurance policies were available to cover the farmer's livestock, but no insurance policies were available to cover the farmer and his family; (c) the farmer was instructed about the methods of proper animal nutrition and schedules of work, but he was not instructed about proper diets and schedules of work for himself and his family; and (d) while a special department was established within the Higher Committee to launch improvement programs for livestock and poultry, no such department was established for the farmer and his family.

Officials of the Higher Committee have always argued that their measures for improving the farmer's economic conditions will automatically improve his social conditions. But because most Egyptian peasants are illiterate and rural life is extremely backward, this argument is not valid. The fact that the farmer's income has increased does not necessarily mean that he will actually devote this increase to the improvement of his level of living through better education, health, housing, and recreation.

The land-reform policy has consisted, so far, of technical and economic approaches to the land problem. Today, there is a great need to implement a social approach to the application of complementary measures in education, health, housing, and the utilization of leisure. Integration of the three approaches into a co-ordinated program requires a systematic procedure. First, special arrangements must be made between the Higher Committee for Agrarian Reform and the Ministries of Education, Public Health, Social Welfare, and other governmental agencies concerned with rural development. Taking into consideration the present highly-organized governmental regime, achievement of this step should not be difficult. Secondly, a special staff must be formed with the sole duty of educating and training all concerned to apply the program. Forming such a staff should not be difficult in view of the considerable number of highly-educated specialists available in Egypt. Thirdly, a local organization capable of carrying out the program must be available in each village. Land-reform co-operative societies can be of considerable help if these are reorganized on new bases that permit their earliest possible independence, and the most active participation of their members. Finally, the program, in order to be effective over long periods, must be explained adequately to the peasants. The Press Department of the Higher Committee issues hundreds of informative publications about land reform. These publications, however, are beyond the comprehension of the illiterate farmers whose only information comes by word of mouth through personal contacts. It is surprising how uninformed the land-reform owners are about matters of their immediate concern. This condition calls for a well-organized information program which must be planned locally and from the farmers' point of view. The program must be designed to answer the questions they want answered, in a language they know and understand. Such a program requires an information officer in each zone to work with the agronomist, the co-operative expert, and the administrator.

II. Trend of the Changes Effected

The crucial question is what the future trend will be in the changes effected as a result of land reform. Because of the short period which has elapsed since the enactment of the Agrarian Reform Law in Egypt, it is difficult to form a clear idea of the prospects for the future. Moreover, the country is undergoing rapid social and economic changes which are bound to influence considerably the results of land reform. Despite this, however, by supplementing the information available at present with the various possible academic approaches to the subject and with the experiences of other countries in earlier land reforms, tentative predictions of the trends can be made.

The recent histories of advanced countries do not provide evidence which suggests that reforms of the agrarian structure have been an essential factor in the process of their development. While some countries have advanced on the basis of equal distribution of ownership, others have used methods of capital accommodations which oppressed small farmers and farm laborers. Switzerland, for example, reached the highest level of living in Europe with peasant systems of farming while England progressed at the expense of her peasant farmers. Warriner compared conditions in Hungary and Bulgaria during the years between the wars. In Hungary, where there had been no land reform, the distribution of land ownership was extremely unequal, about half of the land being in large estates, while about half of the farm population owned no land. Bulgaria had reformed its land system in 1880 by providing for an equal distribution of ownership, with most of the land in small holdings. In comparing the development of the two countries, Warriner stated that Hungary progressed further because the productivity of land and labor there was higher than in Bulgaria, and the wealth of the landlords financed the growth of industry which absorbed the laborers as they were driven off the land. Bulgaria's small farm system tended to keep people working on the land without promoting a high rate of investment.[15]

Land reform in Egypt means more than a mere change in the agrarian structure. It represents a turning point in the nation's history, a crystallization of the determination to break irrevocably with the past. The old land systems have been associated with foreign rules and have been established by foreign conquests. Land reform, therefore, is linked with the achievement of liberation and national independence, which in themselves may inspire further national development. Such development, however, must depend on measures other than land reform. It is very doubtful that the changes effected by land reform in the agrarian structure and the rural social systems will mitigate the problem of excessive population pressure on the land. In Mexico, where land reform has been carried out on an enormous scale, agricultural production and agricultural employment have increased but have not kept pace with the growth of the population. In Egypt, land distribution affected only 6 per cent of the total cultivated area and 3.5 per cent of the total gainfully employed in agriculture. Crop production has increased slightly while some displacement of agricultural laborers has occurred. These results will by no means raise the living standards of the people on the land. Neither are living standards appreciably raised by the transfer of land ownership to the peasants, although changes have been thus effected. Since the transfer the needs of most of them have risen, but has been met by an increase in income; the farmers are happy. They can afford to spend more on tobacco, cigarettes, tea, sugar, and traditional celebrations. But as the families grow in size, and their members grow to adolescence and maturity, their needs will outstrip the income. Sooner or later, the present increase of income will be neutralized.

The possibilities are limited for increasing the value of agricultural products as well as for improving the economic position of the peasant through co-operative organizations. An adequate prediction of the prospects of these organizations cannot be made without consideration of three factors. First, the organizations will not be "co-operative" unless a large measure of voluntary participation and local determination of policies is maintained. Second, the organizations will not succeed in any major way unless they gain the active support of the peasants. Third, the organizations will be limited in their ability to "create" markets, or even to accumulate capital if the members have no surplus. This limitation is affirmed by Thomsen who stated that:

> A century of experience with co-operative marketing offers many valuable lessons to those who will take the trouble to examine. . . . It is quite unreasonable and futile to expect co-operatives to reduce substantially the price or to be largely able to increase returns to members.[16]

Saving and investment are necessary factors for economic development. It is doubtful that the change in the peasants' tenure status will improve their economic conditions. The new owners will continue to possess little savings and, therefore, will be unable to invest in private enterprise. Although their income has increased, a gradual decrease in the rate of saving by the peasants is expected. The new tenure status is creating more needs and more financial responsibilities. The increase of income is creating an additional purchasing power along with a desire to fulfill the new needs, which will affect the prevailing balance between saving and consumption. The trend is likely to be in the direction of more consumption. While there is no prospect of more voluntary saving and investment on the part of the new owners, at the same time, the investment situation will not be substantially worse, for the small cultivators have not been in the habit of investing any considerable proportion of their savings productively.

Investment on the part of former large landowners will somewhat increase. The reform intended to increase investment in land reclamation, mining, and industry by breaking the landlords' desire to hold wealth in the form of land. The original policy was to compensate owners for expropriated land in negotiable bonds in order to achieve this purpose, but since the policy has changed and the bonds are not negotiable, except for the purchase of fallow land from the government, compensation cannot be reinvested in mining or industry. Investment in land reclamation, however, will increase, especially because the Law exempts the land under reclamation from expropriation for twenty-five years.

The abolishment of the strong concentration of landed wealth and the removal of the landlords from their dominating political position will tend to develop democracy in rural Egypt. Large numbers of farm families will have the opportunity to participate freely and openly in political decision-making. In the land-reform areas, because of the obligatory supervised co-operative system, political control from above would be possible in case of crises. This possibility will not be eliminated until after the co-operative organizations are reorganized on new bases that assure their independence and provide for the most active participation of the members.

III. Recommendations

The possibilities of land reform as an aid to social development clearly have definite limitations. In the preceding chapters the analysis of land reform indicated a number of points at which the reform is poorly designed to foster development. The immediate problem then becomes: what measures most intimately connected with social development could be undertaken?

Demographic factors assume major importance along with the basic social and economic factors affecting the welfare of the people in any area. In Egypt, demographic factors constitute a major obstacle to social and economic development. Because of the high birth rate, there are in the population a large number of dependent children in proportion to the number of adults in productive-age groups. The heavy burden of dependent children is somewhat lightened because in the rural areas children begin to work on the farm and become an economic asset at an early age. This early employment, however, is an obstacle to an adequate program of education.

As has been shown, Egypt is primarily agricultural, with a high population density on a limited cultivated area, and with a rising rate of population growth due to high birth rates and to declining, though still high, death rates. This combination of circumstances creates an urgent need for an effective population policy. Broadly outlined, such policy must entail measures for: (a) increasing the area under cultivation, (b) promoting industrialization, and (c) reducing the population growth.

INCREASING THE AREA UNDER CULTIVATION

Increasing the amount of arable land is limited by the amount of water regularly available and by the difficulty of bringing water to some areas.

Achieving cultivation of the largest area possible has always been the foremost goal of the authorities concerned. Land reclamation projects are already underway and are receiving the full support of the government. These projects aim at the reclamation of 321,000 feddans by means of irrigation, drainage, and installation of public utilities.

The greatest undertaking for increasing the cultivated area will be the building of the High Dam near Aswan. This dam will create an artificial lake for the storage of about 130,000,000,000 cubic meters of water, or twenty-four times the present storage capacity of the Aswan Dam. The project will cost about £E 209,000,000, and will provide a hydroelectric station with a capacity of ten billion kilowatt hours and a power transmission line to Cairo about five hundred miles to the north. When the first stage is completed in ten years, this project will increase the water supply for the irrigation of an additional 1,300,000 feddans and the conversion of 700,000 feddans of basin land to perennial irrigation. Thus, in ten years the area now under cultivation is expected to increase by one-third. During the same period, however, the total population is expected to increase by five or six million, which means that the prospective increase in the cultivated area will hardly meet the needs of the prospective increase in population.[17]

PROMOTING INDUSTRIALIZATION

A country as thickly populated as Egypt cannot hope to solve its population problem by agricultural expansion alone. It is believed that a fairly extensive and rapid industrialization is essential to overcome the limitations incident to agricultural expansion. The most general advantages of industrialization are those of increased national productivity and economic opportunity, and the changes in reproductive behavior that may follow the urbanization and secularization of the social structure. The relationship between industrialization and lowered birth rates means that industry not only provides an avenue for support of an expanding population, but helps to introduce those social changes that ease the burden of dependent children on society.[18]

It is mistakenly thought that the problem faced by Egypt in seeking industrial development can be solved by reproducing the conditions that accumulated for Western industrialization. The pattern of historical change which occurred in the West, and is regarded by Western scholars as "natural," will almost certainly not be repeated in Egypt or elsewhere. Moreover, influenced by the world's modern forms of economic organization, new industrialization will not be simply a recapitulation of the past. The accumulated experiences of industrial countries can be used only in making possible more rapid industrialization.

The problem faced by Egypt in seeking industrial development must be solved with consideration of its particular circumstances. First, the unplanned growth of small industries established by private initiative is too slow for the present conditions. Secondly, a planned rapid program of industrialization implies a considerable measure of governmental direction and sponsorship. Governmental sponsorship of industrialization presupposes internal and external political stability. It also presupposes a large measure of international co-operation, often attempted by the Egyptian Government but thwarted by jealous opposition from the great powers. Finally, industrial development requires specific organization of resources and potentialities, capital, and labor. This organization must be examined in relation to industrialization already in process, and in relation to means for more rapid industrialization.[19]

Resources and potentialities. The major industrial centers of the world have been built around abundant natural power, chiefly coal, and accessibility to raw material and markets. In these respects, Egypt is poorly situated.

With respect to natural power, no coal has been discovered in Egypt; the main source of power is petroleum. The price of coal, all of which is imported, is more than twice as high as in the United States. The price of petroleum, however, is quite reasonable; hence the shift away from coal to oil and to electricity generated from oil.[20]

The High Dam, when completed, will provide cheap hydroelectric power that can replace petroleum. But hydroelectric power cannot compete with coal for heavy industry and is unsuitable for steel production. On the other hand, hydroelectric power is of considerable importance in producing some of the lighter metals, especially aluminum and the alloys required for the newer varieties of steel. Hydroelectric power is also of growing technical importance in the development of the light and somewhat decentralized industry for which Egypt is best suited.

With respect to raw materials, it is probable that intensive surveys of the Egyptian deserts will bring to light many unsuspected resources; in this context, the recent discovery of iron ore reserves is significant. At present, however, very few local minerals are available for industry, and most of the minerals that were discovered in the deserts cannot be profitably extracted because of the lack of water and roads. The most readily available raw materials are those originating in agriculture, such as cotton, sugar cane, vegetables, fruits, and milk. All of these, with the exception of cotton, have considerable qualitative and quantitative deficiences.[21] The intensification of farming and the improved agricultural methods, however, can be expected to remedy such deficiences.

With respect to marketing, the poverty of the mass of the population and the preference of the richer classes for foreign goods severely limit the domestic market. Since exports absorb only a negligible fraction of the industrial output, the narrowness of the domestic market limits industrial expansion.[22] The marketing organizations have been improving, following the enactment of measures aiming at improving the quality of Egyptian products, raising the duties on foreign goods, and increasing the purchasing power of the lower classes.

With respect to transportation, the present facilities are extremely inadequate for the transport of raw material to factory centers and of finished goods to the market. The obstacles to a developed transportation system are to be found in the economic structures and can be removed with the modernization of those structures.

Capital. Limited natural resources limit industrial development even under favorable conditions. And when substantial capital is not available for industrial expansion, the conditions cannot be regarded as favorable.

The agricultural organization in Egypt allows little capital accumulation, particularly in the form of cash savings. Consequently, the capital required for government industrialization programs can be obtained only through: (a) taxation, or (b) the export of foodstuffs and the import of capital goods rather than consumer goods, or (c) the import of foreign capital, or (d) the nationalization of industries owned by foreigners.

The first two methods—taxation and securing imports of capital goods—will result in a tremendous reduction in the level of living. The third method—the import of foreign capital—although it does not reduce the level of living, has the disadvantage of imposing specific political agreements. The fourth method—the nationalization of industries owned by foreigners—was adopted by the Egyptian Government.

Labor. Egypt has a large amount of hidden unemployment in agriculture. Part of the farm population is not contributing to agricultural output and is sustained by those who do contribute. Consequently, there is no quantitative shortage for industrial employment. In fact the shifting of agricultural workers to more productive employment is the immediate advantage offered by industrialization. Two qualifications must be noted, however: (a) the quantitative abundance of labor does not mean an immediate availability of appropriate technical skills, and (b) the present locations of supplies of labor are not necessarily suitable locations for industrial establishments. Industrial development will still require a continuous supply of skilled labor, and the transfer of peasants from the villages to factory centers.

Supplying Egyptian industry with skilled labor means that a larger percentage of the people must receive general education for a longer period than at present. This general education must be supplemented by free technical education and industrial recruiting programs. Only by recruiting, educating, and training workers for new occupations will the quantitative supply of labor, which is certainly adequate, have the appropriate skills.

The transfer of peasants from the villages to factory centers depends on both the extent of employment opportunities outside agriculture and the attractiveness of these opportunities. A barely calculative difference in income will not be a sufficient incentive for the peasant to move to a factory center. The attractiveness of industrial employment must be great enough to overcome the intrinsic barriers to mobility, such as kinship ties, property interests, and the pull to the familiar. The new opportunities must provide more security and a higher income than that enjoyed by the peasant, in order to increase his willingness to accept industrial jobs without substantial economic and social loss.

Weighing of all the factors discussed—power, resources, markets, transportation, capital, and labor—suggests that Egypt's potential power resources are not sufficient for the development of heavy industry, with the exception of the domestic processing or industrial exploitation of petroleum resources; hence industrialization programs should be directed toward promoting and expanding the decentralized lighter industries, such as the manufacture of standard consumer goods, building materials, machine tools, precision instruments, and the processing of foodstuffs.

The expansion of decentralized industry may bring about the process of secularization, that is, the breaking down of particular ties and the affiliation of the individual with larger and more specialized groups. The family and the village may cease to be the focus of social life, while occupational and similar groups gain in social and individual importance. The family's role in the individual's emotional life may be enhanced, but its role as the center of his activities may decline. The process of secularization usually results in increased deliberate control of fertility and mortality. Essentially the change stems from more emphasis on individualistic values conducive to small families and the extension of public health and private medical care.[23]

REDUCING THE POPULATION GROWTH

Measures for increasing the area under cultivation and for promoting industrialization will not solve all the demographic, social, and economic problems of Egypt. It is doubtful that even the success of all the measures to increase resources will be sufficient to keep pace with the rapid growth of population or to raise the existing levels of living. The problem of population growth needs a special solution; namely, a turn in the population trends in order to slow down the rapid rate of growth. Many scholars have frequently discussed various solutions. Emigration, especially to less populated Arab countries, has been proposed as a relief from population pressure. Those who support this proposal argue that emigration will reduce the size of the age groups comprised not only of consumers but also of over-abundant laborers and reproducers of the population. Those who oppose this proposal argue that emigrants will be chiefly young, educated adults; hence the country will bear the social and educational costs of dependent children only to lose their productive and military capacities as adults.

The author believes that emigration will not appreciably change the rate of population increase in Egypt. In fact, large-scale emigration may even raise the rate of natural increase since it will make possible a somewhat lower death rate. The birth rate is unlikely to be affected except when a large number of young women emigrate. As stated by Thompson, "People having very high birth rates and high to very high death rates will almost immediately fill any gap left by emigration because of a slight reduction in the death rate."[24]

Even when it is argued that emigration might provide a measure for equalizing economic opportunities, present and probably future conditions make the movement of people on a scale necessary for appreciable results rather impossible. Barriers to immigration have been erected by nearly all of the potential receiving countries, including those of the Arabs, and there seems to be no prospect of reducing these barriers. The most obvious solution for the problem of population growth in Egypt is to develop necessary measures for voluntary control of conception.

From time immemorial, many people have been concerned with the control of the size of their groups. Infanticide, abortion, killing of the aged, marriage restrictions, and sexual taboos have been among the common restrictive practices throughout the greater part of human history. These practices, however, have generally been unconscious and according to custom rather than a result of deliberate individual choice for population control.[25] At present, the development of voluntary contraceptive methods is regarded as one of the major events in human history. Thus, as stated by Thompson:

> For the first time it has become possible for man to achieve a relatively easy and painless adjustment of numbers to the social and economic conditions prevailing at any given time. In the past even when a fairly satisfactory adjustment of numbers to the means of subsistence was achieved, it was done by methods which entailed far more suffering and hardship than does the voluntary control of conception. Think of the suffering and hardship involved in abortion and infanticide and, when "nature" was allowed to take its course, the terrible toll of infant mortality and hunger and epidemics.[26]

Apart from the general rural conservatism of the masses that offers resistance to every change, there is no organized opposition for the voluntary control of conception in Egypt. The issue has neither been completely ignored by the government nor has it been directly opposed by the Islam religion. A question was submitted to the Mufti, the supreme religious teacher of Egypt, as follows:

> A married man to whom one child was born is afraid that if several other children are born he would experience great hardship in rearing and providing for them, and he might suffer a nervous breakdown as a result of his exertions and worries. Or, he may be afraid lest his wife's health might deteriorate as a result of repeated and frequent childbirths, without sufficient interval for birth and recuperation. Now, should he or his wife, under such circumstances, be allowed to take certain measures, recommended by medical men, to avoid frequent childbearing so that a long interval

> may pass between one childbirth and the next, in order that the mother may be rested and the father spared of any undue hardship?

After a careful and detailed examination, particularly in the light of the Hanafy School of Religion, the Grand Mufti, on January 25, 1937, issued his "fatwa" which stated that:

> It is permissible for either husband or wife by mutual consent to take any measures . . . [refers to both natural and artificial methods] . . . in order to prevent conceptions. Scholars of the Hanafy School consider that such consent is not even necessary if either husband or wife has an excuse as those mentioned or any similar.[27]

It should not be a hard task, therefore, to introduce a program in Egypt to encourage family planning and the limitation of the number of children. The public mind should be enlightened as to the benefits of voluntary control of conception. Mothers should be educated to bear children "by choice and not by chance." Facilities for giving advice on contraception should be provided and the advice should be given on medical grounds. Such a program must be particularly active in the villages where the majority of the people live and should not be confined to big cities.

There are, of course, certain specific difficulties which should be taken into consideration before planning and introducing such a program. It should be recognized that the majority of the rural people live in backward conditions. Matters like bathrooms, running water, privacy, illiteracy, poverty, and the reliability, availability, and cheapness of contraceptives need serious attention. Factors such as social and moral attitudes, family structure, and patterns of sexual behavior are bound to influence the readiness for, or resistance to, the voluntary practice of contraception.

While family planning is intended to decrease the rate of population growth over a period of time, it is immediately a step for improving the health of mothers and children. Frequent childbirths undermine the health of the mother, and under conditions of poverty and malnutrition a high birth rate is inevitably connected with a high infant mortality rate and a high incidence of disease among children. Family planning is, therefore, a vital step in social and economic development.[28] Some of the scholars concerned with the population problem of Egypt maintain that there is no need for planning a program for "birth control." Judging by the European experience, they argue, a rise in "culture" is generally followed by a decline in the birth rate. Once the people come to enjoy a high standard of living, the desire to maintain this new standard will lead them to voluntarily restrict the size of their families. The matter of population increase will thus take care of itself.

Very recently, in a newspaper interview, President Nasser was asked, "Is there any idea of introducing birth control with a view to lessening the pressure of overpopulation?" The President replied:

> I am not a believer in calling on people to exercise birth control by decrees or persuasion.
>
> Instead of teaching people how to exercise birth control, we would do better to teach them how to increase their land production and raise their standard. Every one of them will then be able to make his own plans for his own family. In my opinion, instead of concentrating on birth control, we would do better to concentrate on how to make use of our own resources. We live in and make use of only four per cent of the area of our country. The rest is all neglected and desert. If we direct our efforts to expanding the area in which we live instead of concentrating on how to reduce the population, we will soon find the solution.[29]

In this case, the question then becomes: Can Egypt afford to wait until its area is expanded, the level of living is raised, and the desire of the people for family planning is aroused?

IV. Conclusions

The present study has been confined to a relatively narrow sector of the total social situation in Egypt, although the relevance of elements other than those directly discussed has been indicated at numerous junctures. The subject of land reform in relation to social development of the farm population has been treated by examining different sets of conditions and analyzing various aspects of rural life. This treatment necessitated a study of the pattern of land holding and use, the legal and customary institutions of land tenure, the structure and function of rural social systems, and the social, economic, and political forces which worked for or against social change.

A study of this kind can never be definitive and complete. Problems and situations which arose during the short period of observation may persist unaltered for long periods of time; they may become intensified; they may pale into insignificance; or they may be solved by measures which come into operation afterwards. Thus abstraction is less crucial to an analysis of demographic, social, and economic circumstances than to the drawing of conclusions.

The analysis developed here indicates that land reform has very definite limitations as an aid to the social development of the farm population in Egypt. The purpose of land reform was to distribute the already available wealth rather than to produce new additional wealth. The process of social development tends to depend on the rate of population growth in its relation to the expansion of the cultivated area and the creation of employment alternatives to agriculture. Land reform has neither checked the population growth nor compensated for the lack of land and industry. It has modified, however, the institutional framework of the society and has established situations favorable to social change. This modification is an essential first step to the process of social development. It must be followed by other steps for reducing the rate of population growth, increasing the social well-being of the people, and preparing the peasants to overcome centuries of deprivation. These steps may or may not be achieved in a manner satisfactory to all those whose interests and aspirations are involved. Some solutions seem possible, however, if the appropriate course of action is taken and the affected people are willing to endure the inevitable sacrifices of traditional values. The main point to be emphasized is that land reform, by itself, does not suffice to raise the levels of living or arouse the desire of the peasants to achieve and maintain higher living standards.

It can be concluded, therefore, that although land reform does not necessarily create a condition of social development, it is certainly a key to this development.

Appendix

METHODOLOGY

THE UNIVERSE

Briefly stated, the universe in this study consists of farm families in rural Egypt who acquired ownership of agricultural land according to the provisions of the Agrarian Reform Law of 1952. The Law sets two hundred feddans as a maximum limit of ownership, and empowers the government to make a requisition on land holdings in excess of this limit within a period of five years. Article nine of the Law stipulates that the land requisitioned should be distributed among small peasants, so that each one of them should have a small holding of not fewer than two feddans and not more than five feddans. Official figures published by the Higher Committee for Agrarian Reform indicate that up to the end of 1955, an area of 206,792 feddans were distributed among 68,156 farm families in rural Egypt. A breakdown of these figures by year of distribution shows that in 1953 an area of 18,402 feddans was distributed among 4,315 families; in 1954 an area of 82,897 feddans was distributed among 24,038 families; and in 1955 an area of 105,493 feddans was distributed among 39,803 families.

SAMPLE AREA

The sample in this study was not intended to be a representative cross section of the population of rural communities throughout Egypt, but only a sample of the farmers who acquired ownership of land according to the provisions of the Agrarian Reform Law of 1952. It is, therefore, a sample of a specialized group and should be interpreted as such.

Because of the short period which has elapsed since the enactment of the Law, field studies were concentrated upon land-reform farmers who acquired land ownership during the first year of distribution. It was thought that a study of these farmers and their families might show the social changes effected more clearly than a study of any other group of farm families that could be made.

The land distributed in 1953, the first year of distribution, is located in three estates at the northern part of Lower Egypt. The three estates are: Demera in Dakahlia Province, Zafaran in Kafr El-Sheik Province, and Maania in Behira Province. Examination of official registries in these estates indicated considerable error in the figures published by the Higher Committee for Agrarian Reform. Official registries indicate that 12,739 feddans were distributed in 1953, while the corresponding figure published by the Higher Committee was 18,402. Official registries also listed 3,920 as the total number of farmers who acquired ownership of this land, while the corresponding figure published by the Higher Committee was 4,315. Table 1 indicates the discrepancies between these figures.

Although the Agrarian Reform Law stipulates that the requisitioned land should be distributed in holdings of not fewer than two feddans and not more than five feddans, the figures published by

TABLE 1

Land Distributed in 1953 and Number of Farmers Who Acquired its Ownership

Estate	Figures obtained from official registries*			Figures published by H.C.A.R.**		
	Area (feddans)	Number of owners	Average size of holding (feddans)	Area (feddans)	Number of owners	Average size of holding (feddans)
Demera	9521	2892	3.29	11988	3033	3.95
Zafaran	2487	792	3.14	5051	973	5.19
Maania	731	236	3.10	1363	309	4.41
Total	12739	3920	3.18	18402	4315	4.52

*Combined by the author from the estates' official registries.

**Published by Higher Committee for Agrarian Reform, Press Department.

the Higher Committee indicate that the average of holdings distributed in Demera, Zafaran, and Maania estates is 4.0, 5.2, and 4.4 feddans, respectively. Since the land was actually distributed in holdings of from two to five feddans according to the Law, these averages seem considerably higher than should be expected. On the other hand, figures for the average size of holdings obtained from official registries in the three estates seem quite reliable.

In view of the unreliability of the figures published by the Higher Committee, data obtained from the official registries of the estates were used to avoid any inaccuracy or lack of uniformity.

SIZE AND DISTRIBUTION OF SAMPLE

The land-reform owners are to a considerable degree a homogeneous group. They are all Egyptians, of age, not convicted of any criminal charges, working in agriculture, and own fewer than five feddans of agricultural land. Moreover, at least within each estate, these owners and their families have common cultural backgrounds, historical circumstances, physical environments, and socio-economic characteristics.

It was therefore estimated that a sample of three hundred land-reform owners would fairly represent the universe and serve as a reliable base for statistical manipulations. The number of cases needed for the sample was equally distributed among the three estates in the sample area. A proportionate distribution according to the number of owners in each estate would have been inadequate for two reasons: First, the number of farmers who acquired land in 1953 was not the product of any characteristic of the estates, but was strictly determined by the distribution policy for that year. A proportionate distribution would have had no significance. Secondly, the number of farmers who acquired land in 1953 on Zafaran and Maania estates was relatively small in comparison to the number on Demera estate. A proportionate distribution would not have provided a sufficient number of cases for an adequate analysis with respect to the characteristics of the farmers in Zafaran and Maania estates.

Therefore, on each estate, a stratified random sample of one hundred farmers was drawn from those who acquired ownership of land in 1953. The estate official registries contain information about land-reform beneficiaries, the date when land was distributed to them, the location of each holding, the sizes of their farms, and the sizes of their families. The sizes of farms appeared to be the most significant variable as a criterion for stratifying the owners on each estate. According to the distribution plan, the size of farms assigned to land-reform owners was calculated on the basis of a large number of factors including size of family, ages of family members, estimated cost of living per family, and productivity per feddan of land distributed. Therefore, a stratification based on size of farm would actually be based on all those factors combined. Table 2

TABLE 2

Distribution of the 1953 Land-Reform Owners by Size of Farm

Estate	Total owners of 1953		Owners of 2-3 feddans		Owners of 3-4 feddans		Owners of 4-5 feddans	
	Number	Per cent	Number	Per cent	Number	Per cent	Number	Per cent
Demera	2892	100	1272	44	1099	38	521	18
Zafaran	792	100	404	51	253	32	135	17
Maania	236	100	118	50	85	36	33	14
Total	3920	100	1794	45.8	1437	36.6	689	17.6

Source: Combined by author from estates' official registries.

shows the distribution of the 1953 land-reform owners by size of farm. Owners in each class interval were arranged alphabetically and numbered consecutively. The needed sample was then drawn by a set of random numbers. The percentage of owners in each class interval determined the number of cases to be drawn from that class. For example, in Demera estate, 44 per cent of the owners acquired two to three feddans, 38 per cent acquired over three to four feddans, and 18 per cent acquired over four to five feddans. Consequently, forty-four, thirty-eight, and eighteen owners were drawn by random, respectively, from these class intervals to form the one hundred owners needed for the sample in this estate. The same procedure was followed for Zafaran and Maania estates in order to secure a sample representing proportionate numbers of farmers in each class interval. Table 3 shows the sample distribution on each estate.

TABLE 3

Distribution of Sampling Units

Estate	Total in Sample	Owners of 2-3 feddans	Owners of 3-4 feddans	Owners of 4-5 feddans
Demera	100	44	38	18
Zafaran	100	51	32	17
Maania	100	50	36	14
Total	300	145	106	49

THE SURVEY PHASE

A matched-estate survey was conducted to evaluate the differences in changes effected in two related areas during the period from 1952 to 1956. Three Wakf estates were selected, each as a control for one of the land-reform estates in the sample area. Shawa estate was selected as a control for Demera estate, Beyala as a control for Zafaran, and Saft Khaled as a control for Maania.

Because the land in the three control estates was mortmain property which had been dedicated to religious institutions and for charitable purposes, it was inalienable; it could not be sold, transferred, or mortgaged. It could, however, be exchanged for other property of similar value, and it could be rented. The Ministry of Wakf, which supervised the management of these estates, rented the land to small tenant-cultivators in the area. When the Agrarian Reform Law was enacted, the control estates were exempt from expropriation and redistribution measures. The tenant-cultivators remained on the land without acquiring its ownership or changing their tenure status.

The matching between the land-reform estates and the control estates was in respect to the following factors:

1. Geographical location
2. Cultural background
3. Physical setting
4. Agrarian structure in 1952
5. Structure of rural social systems in 1952

The following factors were items of the survey:

I. Changes in agrarian structure during the period from 1952 to 1956
   A. Tenure status
   B. Tenancy conditions
   C. Size of farming units
   D. Type of farming
   E. Farming techniques
   F. Farming supplies
   G. Organization of agricultural production
   H. Crop marketing
   I. Credit facilities
   J. Agricultural development projects

II. Changes in rural social systems
   A. The rural family
   B. The village
   C. Rural social strata
   D. Political and governmental systems
   E. Educational systems
   F. Rural service agencies
      1. Extension service
      2. Rural health and medical care
      3. Social welfare service

The data for the survey were obtained from the following sources:

1. Estates' official registries and records
2. Personal interviews with government representatives on the estates, civil service personnel, and conferences with other government agencies
3. Personal interviews with key leaders in the communities

4. Government and non-government publications
5. Census returns
6. Vital statistics records
7. Special case studies

THE INTERVIEW PHASE

Matched-family interviews were conducted to isolate and measure accurately by empirical means the difference between the socio-economic levels of two groups. A group of land-reform owners in the sample was matched with a similar size group of tenant-cultivators from the three control estates. The first group consisted of three hundred farm families who were tenant-cultivators before 1952, and acquired ownership of the land according to the provisions of the Agrarian Reform Law. The second group consisted of three hundred farm families who were also tenant-cultivators before 1952, but did not acquire ownership of land after the enactment of the Law. These families remained on the land without any changes in their tenure status. The first group was termed "Land-Reform Owners," and the second group was termed "Non-Land-Reform Tenant-Cultivators."

The matching of the two groups was in respect to the following factors:

1. Area of location
2. Tenure status in 1952
3. Size of farm in 1956
4. Size of family in 1956
5. Sibling position in 1956
6. Age and sex of family head
7. Education of family head

Interviews were then conducted with family heads in the two groups. Association of each group with the following factors were items of interview:

1. General background
2. Economic conditions
3. Mutual-help arrangements and farming operations
4. Health and medical care
5. Education and communication media
6. Housing conditions
7. Recreation and utilization of leisure

8. Organizational participation
9. Attitudes toward family life
10. Attitudes toward land reform

Focused interviews were used to secure the needed information. Each interview proceeded on the basis of a schedule constructed in English to outline areas of inquiry. A first pretest indicated certain weaknesses in the schedule with respect to some areas in which it seemed difficult to get responses. The farmers were unable to express themselves and usually used terms which could not be translated into the English language. The schedule was then revised and check-response items were used instead of free responses. A second pretest indicated the adequacy of the revised schedule and there was no difficulty in getting the needed information or in translating the responses.

The revised schedule appears on pages 117-123.

Estate No. ____________ Date of Interview ____________
Sample No. ____________ Interview Completed ____________
Schedule No. ____________ Interview Refused ____________

General Background

1. Age, sex, and education of family members (1956)

Name	Age	Sex	Education	Relation to head
1. ____________	___	___	________	________
2. ____________	___	___	________	________
3. ____________	___	___	________	________
4. ____________	___	___	________	________
5. ____________	___	___	________	________
6. ____________	___	___	________	________
7. ____________	___	___	________	________
8. ____________	___	___	________	________
9. ____________	___	___	________	________
10. ____________	___	___	________	________

2. Size of farm in 1956 ________ feddans
3. Size of farm in 1952 ________ feddans
4. Tenure status in 1956
   a. Owner-cultivator _____ c. Tenant _____
   b. Tenant-owner _____ d. Agricultural worker _____
5. Tenure status in 1952
   a. Owner-cultivator _____ c. Tenant _____
   b. Tenant-owner _____ d. Agricultural worker _____
6. Size of family in 1956 _____
7. Size of family in 1952 _____

Economic Conditions

1. Net income from field crops in 1956 _____ £E
2. Net income from field crops in 1952 _____ £E

3. Net income from livestock and poultry in 1956 ____ £E
4. Net income from livestock and poultry in 1952 ____ £E
5. Total net income from farming in 1956 ____ £E
6. Total net income from farming in 1952 ____ £E
7. Value of livestock and poultry in 1956 ____ £E
8. Value of livestock and poultry in 1952 ____ £E
9. Family expenses on meat in 1956 ____ £E
10. Family expenses on clothes in 1956 ____ £E
11. Family expenses on tea, coffee, cigarettes, tobacco in 1956 ____ £E
12. Family expenses on traditional celebrations in 1956 ____ £E
13. Were items on expenses purchased in cash? yes____ no____
14. Were you in debt in 1956? yes____ no____
15. Were you in debt in 1952? yes____ no____

Mutual-help Arrangements and Farming Operations

1. Did unpaid family members help in your farming operations in 1956? yes____ no____
2. Did unpaid family members help in your farming operations in 1952? yes____ no____
3. Did unpaid relatives (other than family members) help in your farming operations in 1956? yes____ no____
4. Did unpaid relatives (other than family members) help in your farming operations in 1952? yes____ no____
5. Did unpaid neighbors (other than relatives) help in your farming operations in 1956? yes____ no____
6. Did unpaid neighbors (other than relatives) help in your farming operations in 1952? yes____ no____
7. Did you use chemical fertilizer on your farm in 1956? yes____ no____
8. Did you use chemical fertilizer on your farm in 1952? yes____ no____

9. Did you use selected seeds on your farm in 1956? yes____ no____
10. Did you use selected seeds on your farm in 1952? yes____ no____
11. Did you use agricultural machinery on your farm in 1956? yes____ no____
12. Did you use agricultural machinery on your farm in 1952? yes____ no____
13. Sources of farm supplies in 1956
    a. Cooperative societies___ c. Local market ___
    b. Landlords or managers___ d. Other sources(specify)___
    ____
14. Sources of farm supplies in 1952
    a. Cooperative societies___ c. Local market ___
    b. Landlords or managers___ d. Other sources(specify)___
    ____
15. Sources of loans in 1956
    a. Cooperative societies___ d. Other sources(specify)___
    b. Landlords or managers___ ______________________
    c. Usurers ___ e. No sources ___
16. Per cent interest paid on loans in 1956 ___
17. Sources of loans in 1952
    a. Cooperative societies___ d. Other sources(specify)___
    b. Landlords or managers___ ______________________
    c. Usurers ___ e. No sources ___
18. Per cent interest paid on loans in 1952 ___
19. Marketing crops in 1956
    a. Through cooperative societies ___
    b. Through landlords or managers ___
    c. Through local market ___
    d. Through other agencies(specify)______________________
20. Marketing of crops in 1952
    a. Through cooperative societies ___

b. Through landlords or managers ____
c. Through local market ____
d. Through other agencies(specify)________________

Health and Medical Care

1. Where do you and your family usually go for treatment when sick?
   a. Public hospitals ____
   b. Private clinic ____
   c. Non-Professional Practitioner ____
   d. Barber ____
   e. Wise neighbors for advice____
   f. Other places (specify) ____ ________________
   g. No place ____
2. Attitudes toward public hospitals
   a. No particular feeling ____
   b. Feeling of security ____
   c. No proper care at public hospitals ____
   d. Care as well at home ____
   e. Suspicious of public hospitals ____
   f. Hostility against public hospitals ____
   g. Other feelings(specify)____ ________________

Education and Communication Media

1. Number of children who were in school in 1956 ____
2. Education of head
   a. Illiterate ____
   b. Attended illiteracy campaign ____
   c. Attended El-Kottab____
   d. Attended elementary school ____
   e. Attended schools superior to Elementary ____
3. Do you have a radio set? yes____ no____
4. Do you listen in to radio? yes____ no____
5. If yes, what programs do you prefer?
   a. Koran ____
   e. Rural programs ____

b. News ____ f. Lectures and talks ____
c. Songs and music ____ g. Other programs(specify)__
d. Plays and stories ____ ______________________

Housing Conditions

1. Construction of house
   a. Mud brick ____ c. Stone ____
   b. Brick ____ d. Others (specify) ____
   ____
2. Number of rooms in house____
3. Number of persons living in house____
4. Water piped into house yes____ no____
5. Bathroom in house yes____ no____
6. Changes that took place in house since 1952
   a. No changes ____ d. Addition of rooms ____
   b. Painting ____ e. Remodeling ____
   c. Repairing ____ f. Other changes(specify)___
   ____

Recreation and Utilization of Leisure

1. Where do you spend leisure time?
   a. At own home ____ e. At gathering places ____
   b. At friends' homes ____ f. Idling ____
   c. At coffee shops ____ g. Others (specify) ____
   d. At village mosque ____ ______________________
2. Recreational activities preferred
   a. Outdoor sports ____ e. Gossiping and conversations ____
   b. Outdoor games ____
   c. Indoor games ____ f. Celebrations ____
   d. Social gatherings ____ g. Listening to radio ____
   h. Other activities(specify)
   ____

Organizational Participation

1. Were you a member of a cooperative society in 1952?
   yes____ no____
2. Were you a member of a cooperative society in 1956?
   yes____ no____
3. If yes, were you satisfied with services rendered in 1956? yes____ no____
4. Confidence in cooperative's officers and officials
   Complete confidence____ Little confidence____
   Some confidence ____ No confidence ____
5. Services expected from cooperative society other than those rendered
   a. Social services ____
   b. Recreational ____
   c. Medical services ____
   d. Welfare services ____
   e. Educational services ____
   f. Industrialization ____
   g. Other services(specify)___ ________________________
   h. None ____

Attitudes Toward Family Life

1. Are you in favor of early marriages or late marriages?
   Early____ Late____
2. Are you in favor of large families or small families?
   Large____ Small____
3. Number of children preferred______
4. Sex of children preferred
   a. All boys ____
   b. All girls ____
   c. Mostly boys ____
   d. Mostly girls ____
   e. Boys as well as girls ____
   f. Sex makes no difference____
5. Are you in favor of regarding boys as superior to girls in status? yes____ no____
6. Have you heard of birth control? yes____ no____
7. If yes, are you in favor of practicing contraception methods? yes____ no____

8. Are you in favor of having more than one wife? yes____ no____
9. Are you in favor of divorce being only through courts? yes____ no____
10. Are you in favor of married sons living in the same house with parents? yes____ no____
11. Are you in favor of giving daughters freedom to choose their husbands? yes____ no____
12. Are you in favor of giving sons freedom to choose their wives? yes____ no____
13. Are you in favor of educating girls? yes____ no____
14. Are you in favor of girls working away from home? yes____ no____

Attitudes Toward Land Reform

(These questions are asked only of land-reform owners)

1. Was land reform beneficial to your village? yes____ no____
2. Was land reform beneficial to your family? yes____ no____
3. If there had been no land reform, how do you think living conditions in your village would have been?
   Better____ Worse____ Same____
4. If there had been no land reform, how do you think living conditions in your family would have been?
   Better____ Worse____ Same____
5. How are living conditions in your family as compared with them before land reform?
   Better____ Worse____ Same____
6. Was the method of determining who was eligible to purchase land appropriate? yes____ no____
7. Was the land you purchased enough for family needs? yes____ no____
8. Do you prefer to be as you were before land reform? yes____ no____
9. Are you pleased to be an owner under land reform? yes____ no____

THE FIELD WORK

The Population Council Fellowship enabled the author to travel to Egypt and conduct the needed field work from September, 1956, to August, 1957. The Minister of State for Agrarian Reform and other personnel were contacted initially and the nature and purpose of the study was explained to them. Consequently, the author was issued a free railroad pass for traveling, and a permit for living in land-reform rest houses. Official personnel in each estate were instructed to assist the author, facilitate his work, and provide him with the needed records and registries.

The field work was not an easy task. It required, above all, deep understanding and sincere appreciation of farm people and their value systems. Egyptian farm people are usually simple, suspicious, talkative, and illiterate. Their value systems are usually based on their religion, their village, and their families, rather than on the individual. Because the author is a native Egyptian and had lived and worked with farmers for several years, he was able to secure more easily the cooperation of the interviewees and thus facilitate the field studies.

The first step in field work was a general study of the area of investigation, involving careful examination of official registries, estate records, census returns, and government publications. Several meetings were held with government representatives, administrative personnel, and local leaders, during which the purpose of the study was explained and arrangements were made for field work. This step familiarized the author with the data available from ordinary sources, and enabled him to gather some clues about the prospective interviewees.

The second step in the field work was to evaluate by several case studies the changes between 1952 and 1956 in the agrarian structure and the structure of rural social systems. Special interviews were also conducted with several officials and local persons to supplement these case studies. In the meantime, farm families were visited in order to win their confidence and become acquainted with their customs.

The third step in the field work was the interviewing of farm families in the sample. All these families welcomed the author to their homes, and expressed sincere willingness and desire to co-operate. There were some difficulties, however, in conducting the interviews. First, many farmers were unable to express themselves. The use of check-response items in the revised schedule solved this problem. Second, the farmers were neither statistically conscious nor were they aware of dates. They identified factual information by relating it to events of national importance. This problem was solved in part by probing and careful checking of responses. Third, the farmers were very talkative during the interview. Once a question was asked, several stories were told and the author had to be a sympathetic listener, which sometimes made it difficult to control the direction of interviews. Fourth, the farmers were very generous. During each interview strong black tea was served at least three times, followed by a warm bottle of Coca-Cola. Around meal hours, fatty heavy food was usually served. This was the customary way to honor a special guest; to refuse what was offered would have greatly insulted the hosts. At the end of the field work, during which an average of six interviews a day were held, the author was hospitalized for twenty-eight days.

STATISTICAL PROCEDURE

Data obtained from the survey phase were not processed for statistical manipulations and were used only to evaluate the effect of land reform on the rural community as a whole. Data obtained from the interview phase were processed for statistical analysis to test accurately the significance of the difference between the social levels of the "land-reform owners group" and the "non-land-reform tenant-cultivators group." For this purpose, the data were coded from the interview schedules and transferred to IBM punch cards. Cross tabulations were designed for correlating the results with four independent variables: (a) age, (b) size of farm, (c) size of family, and (d) education of family head. It was hypothesized that the land-reform group and the control group were drawn from the same parent population and that, therefore, the coefficient of correlation between the patterns of distribution for the two groups is perfect ($r=1.0$). This hypothesis must be rejected if the true value of the difference between the observed and hypothetical coefficients is significantly different from zero. The statistical procedure followed in this respect can be summarized as follows:

1. Set up the hypothesis that the coefficient of correlation between the patterns of distribution for the two groups is perfect and that the true value of the difference between the observed and hypothetical coefficients is zero.

2. Compute the coefficient of correlation between the observed patterns of distribution for the two groups.

3. Transfer the observed and hypothetical coefficients to their corresponding logarithmic function, z'.

4. Compute the difference between the observed and hypothetical z' values.

5. Test the significance of this difference from zero. This step requires: (a) computation of the standard error of the difference between the observed and hypothetical z' values, (b) computation of the t value for this difference, and (c) interpretation of the significance of the t value at a certain level.

Table 4 indicates the observed coefficients of correlation, r, and the degrees of freedom, n, between the distribution patterns of the farmers in the two groups. Table 5 indicates the t values for the standard error of the difference between the observed and hypothetical coefficients, according to different levels of observed coefficients and given degrees of freedom. In this study, these t values were interpreted at the 1 per cent level of significance.

TABLE 4: Observed Coefficients of Correlation, r, and Degrees of Freedom, n, between the Distribution Patterns of the Farmers in the Land Reform and Control Groups

Correlation between distribution patterns of farmers in the two groups according to:	Observed Coefficients r	Degrees of freedom, n
Size of farm and net revenue from field crops	.25	10
Size of farm and net farm income	.17	11
Age and net farm income	.36	30
Size of family and net farm income	.10	21
Education and net farm income	.68	23
Size of farm and value of livestock	.95	15
Size of family and expense on meat	.89	16
Education and expense on meat	.96	18
Size of family and expense on clothes	.99	16
Education and expense on clothes	.99	17
Size of family and expense on tea and coffee	.19	15
Education and expense on tea and coffee	.68	18
Size of family and expense on traditional celebrations	.23	10
Education and expense on traditional celebrations	.79	13
Age and method of payment for items purchased	.95	8
Size of family and method of payment for items purchased	.97	8

TABLE 4 (Continued)

Correlation between distribution patterns of farmers in the two groups according to:	Observed Coefficients r	Degrees of freedom, n
Education and method of payment for items purchased	.99	9
Education and debt condition	.94	14
Size of farm and mutual-help arrangements	.86	5
Age and mutual-help arrangements	.86	8
Size of family and mutual-help arrangements	.89	8
Education and mutual-help arrangements	.94	9
Age and health attitudes	.99	22
Education and health attitudes	.99	14
Education and number of children in school	.98	11
Age and availability of radio sets	.97	12
Education and availability of radio sets	.99	12
Age and radio programs preferred	.96	23
Education and radio programs preferred	.98	26
Size of family and number of rooms in house	.96	17
Age and changes in house	.99	19
Education and changes in house	.99	18
Age and utilization of leisure time	.90	28
Education and utilization of leisure time	.94	25
Age and recreational activities preferred	.97	14
Education and recreational activities preferred	.98	14
Age and attitudes toward marriage	.94	8
Education and attitudes toward marriage	.99	6
Age and attitudes toward divorce	.99	6
Education and attitudes toward divorce	.99	8
Age and attitudes toward size of family	.93	8
Education and attitudes toward size of family	.98	6
Age and sex of children preferred	.92	14
Education and sex of children preferred	.98	15
Age and attitudes toward birth control	.99	12
Education and attitudes toward birth control	.99	16
Age and attitudes toward choice of spouses	.96	8
Education and attitudes toward choice of spouses	.99	6
Age and attitudes toward education of girls	.92	8
Education and attitudes toward education of girls	.98	6

TABLE 5. Value of t for the Difference Between the Observed and Hypothetical Coefficients, According to Different Levels of Observed Coefficients of Correlation, r, with Given Degrees of Freedom, n *

Degrees of Freedom n	Observed Coefficients of Correlation, r									
	.50	.55	.60	.65	.70	.75	.80	.85	.90	.95
5	2.28	2.20	2.12	2.03	1.93	1.82	1.68	1.51	1.27	0.88
6	2.72	2.63	2.53	2.42	2.30	2.17	2.00	1.80	1.52	1.06
7	3.09	2.99	2.88	2.76	2.63	2.47	2.28	2.05	1.73	1.20
8	3.43	3.32	3.20	3.06	2.91	2.74	2.53	2.27	1.92	1.33
9	3.74	3.62	3.48	3.33	3.17	2.98	2.76	2.48	2.09	1.45
10	4.22	3.89	3.75	3.59	3.41	3.21	2.97	2.67	2.25	1.56
11	4.29	4.15	3.99	3.82	3.64	3.42	3.16	2.84	2.40	1.67
12	4.54	4.39	4.22	4.05	3.85	3.62	3.35	3.00	2.54	1.76
13	4.77	4.61	4.44	4.26	4.05	3.81	3.52	3.16	2.67	1.85
14	5.00	4.83	4.65	4.46	4.24	3.99	3.69	3.31	2.80	1.94
15	5.21	5.04	4.86	4.65	4.42	4.16	3.85	3.46	2.92	2.03
16	5.42	5.24	5.05	4.84	4.60	4.32	4.00	3.59	3.03	2.11
17	5.62	5.43	5.23	5.01	4.77	4.48	4.15	3.73	3.15	2.18
18	5.81	5.62	5.41	5.18	4.93	4.64	4.29	3.85	3.25	2.26
19	6.00	5.80	5.59	5.35	5.09	4.79	4.43	3.98	3.36	2.33
20	6.18	5.97	5.75	5.51	5.24	4.93	4.56	4.10	3.46	2.40
21	6.35	6.14	5.92	5.67	5.39	5.07	4.69	4.21	3.56	2.47
22	6.52	6.31	6.08	5.82	5.54	5.21	4.82	4.33	3.65	2.53
23	6.69	6.47	6.23	5.97	5.68	5.34	4.94	4.44	3.75	2.60
24	6.85	6.63	6.38	6.11	5.81	5.47	5.06	4.54	3.84	2.66
25	7.01	6.78	6.53	6.26	5.95	5.60	5.18	4.65	3.93	2.72
26	7.17	6.93	6.68	6.39	6.08	5.72	5.29	4.75	4.01	2.78
27	7.32	7.08	6.82	6.53	6.21	5.84	5.40	4.85	4.10	2.84
28	7.47	7.22	6.96	6.66	6.34	5.96	5.51	4.95	4.18	2.90
29	7.61	7.36	7.09	6.79	6.46	6.08	5.62	5.05	4.26	2.96
30	7.76	7.50	7.22	6.92	6.58	6.19	5.73	5.14	4.34	3.01

*Since the value of z' becomes indefinite when the value of $r=1.0$, the hypothetical coefficient was reduced to .99 in order to make possible the computation of the difference between the observed and hypothetical z' values.

Notes

CHAPTER I

1. Kenneth H. Parsons *et al.*, *Land Tenure* (Madison: University of Wisconsin Press, 1956), p. 17.

2. William D. P. Bliss, "Land Reform," *The New Encyclopedia of Social Reforms* (4th ed.; London: Wagnall's Company, 1908), p. 695.

3. *Ibid.*, p. 694.

4. A. Whitney Griswold, *Farming and Democracy* (New York: Harcourt, Brace and Co., 1948), pp. 138-143.

5. Philip C. Newman, *The Development of Economic Thought* (New York: Prentice-Hall, 1952), p. 157.

6. Karl Marx, *The Poverty of Philosophy* (New York: International Publishers, n.d.), pp. 145-146.

7. A. C. Pigou, *The Economics of Welfare* (London: Macmillan and Co., 1948), pp. 89, 758-67.

8. Leonard A. Salter, Jr., "Do We Need a New Land Policy?" *Readings on Agricultural Policy,* ed. O. B. Jesness (Philadelphia: Blakiston Co., 1949), p. 336.

9. United Nations, *Progress In Land Reform* (New York: U. N. Department of Economic Affairs, 1954), p. iii.

10. *Ibid.*, p. iv.

11. Doreen Warriner, *Land Reform and Economic Development* (Cairo: National Bank of Egypt, 1955), pp. 1-2.

12. United Nations, p. 49.

13. Parsons *et al.*, p. 44.

14. *Ibid.*, p. 4.

15. Doreen Warriner, *Land Reform and Development in the Middle East* (London: Royal Institute of International Affairs, 1957), p. 5.

16. *Ibid.*, p. 6.

17. Parsons *et al.*, p. 25.

18. *Ibid.*, p. 35.

19. Higher Committee for Agrarian Reform, *Land Reform Law Full Text* (Cairo: Press Department, 1954), pp. 3-30.

20. Erich H. Jacoby, *Inter-Relationship Between Agrarian Reform and Agricultural Development* (Rome: Food and Agriculture Organization of the United Nations, 1953), pp. 6-8.

21. *New York Times*, October 18, 1950.

22. Charles F. Brannan, "Agriculture and National Defense," Speech before the United States Department of Agriculture Outlook Conference, Washington, D. C., October 30, 1950.

23. Speech before the United Nations General Assembly, Committee Two, October 31, 1950. The full text is available in *Congressional Record* for December 5, 1950, Appendix, pp. A 7897-98.

24. Speech at El-Krion, Behira Province, Cairo, Egypt, April 19, 1956.

25. Higher Committee for Agrarian Reform, *Replies to the United Nations' Questionnaires Relating to Egyptian Agrarian Reform Measures* (Cairo: Press Department, 1955), pp. 6, 7, 13.

26. Higher Committee for Agrarian Reform, *Demera Estate* (Cairo: Press Department, 1953), p. 20.

CHAPTER II

1. Roland R. Renne, *Land Economics* (New York: Harper and Brothers, 1947), p. 429.

2. Erich H. Jacoby, *Inter-Relationship Between Agrarian Reform and Agricultural Development* (Rome: Food and Agriculture Organization of the United Nations, 1953), p. 9.

3. Inter-Regional Land Tenure Research Committee, *Agricultural Land Tenure Research, Scope and Nature: Reappraisal* (Chicago: Farm Foundation, 1955), p. 2.

4. Kenneth H. Parsons *et al., Land Tenure* (Madison: University of Wisconsin Press, 1956), p. 101.

5. Sayed Marei, *Agrarian Reform in Egypt* (Cairo: Institute of Oriental Archeology Press, 1957), p. 191.

6. *Ibid.*, p. 192.

7. Department of Agriculture, Egypt, *Monthly Agricultural Bulletin*, No. 6, October 1949, p. 16.

8. Mohamed R. Ghonemy, "Resource Use and Income in Egyptian Agriculture Before and After Land Reform with Particular Reference to Economic Development" (unpublished Ph. D. dissertation, North Carolina State College, 1953), p. 57.

9. *Ibid.*, p. 58.

10. Doreen Warriner, *Land Reform and Development in the Middle East* (London: Royal Institute of International Affairs, 1957), p. 27.

11. Marei, p. 168.

12. Ministry of Finance and National Economy, Egypt, *Public Domain Bureau, Its Establishment and Work* (Cairo: Department of Finance, 1949), p. 37.

13. Ghonemy, pp. 53-56.

14. *Ibid.*, pp. 61-62.

15. Charles P. Issawi, *Egypt at Mid-Century, An Economic Survey* (London: Oxford University Press, 1954), pp. 54-55, 61, and 79-80.

16. Bureau of Statistics and Census, Egypt, *Population Census of Egypt, 1947* (Cairo: Government Press, 1954), p. 2.

17. Issawi, pp. 59-60.

18. Ministry of Social Affairs, Egypt, *Second Social Welfare Seminar for Arab States of the Middle East* (Cairo: S.O.P. Press, 1950), p. 405.

19. National Bank of Egypt, *Economic Bulletin*, Vol. VIII, No. 3 (Cairo: Research Department of the Bank, 1955), p. 181.

20. Warriner, p. 19.

21. *Ibid.*, p. 20.

22. Hasan M. Hussein, "Population in Relation to the Development of Agriculture," Paper presented before the World Population Conference, meeting No. 22, Rome, September, 1954.

CHAPTER III

1. Charles P. Issawi, *Egypt at Mid-Century, An Economic Survey* (London: Oxford University Press, 1954), pp. 260-261.

2. Gamayet El-Nahda El-Kawmia, *A Proposed Agrarian Reform* (Cairo: Missr Press, 1948), pp. 13-18.

3. Ahmed Hussein, "Egypt's New Regime" (Washington D. C.: Egyptian Embassy, June, 1953). (Mimeographed.)

4. United Nations, *Progress in Land Reform* (New York: U.N. Department of Economic Affairs, 1954), pp. iii-v.

5. Clarence J. McCormick, "Beyond Today's Horizon," Opening Statement before the Twelfth FAO Council Session, Rome, Italy, June 11, 1951.

6. Kenneth H. Parsons *et al., Land Tenure* (Madison: University of Wisconsin Press, 1956), p. 28.

7. United Nations, pp. 54-59, 71-72, 80.

8. Egyptian Embassy, "Explanatory Note on Land Reform Law" (Washington D.C.: Press Department, December, 1952). (Mimeographed.)

9. Higher Committee for Agrarian Reform, *Changes in the Institutional Structure which Form an Obstacle to Agricultural Development in Egypt* (Cairo: Press Department, 1957), pp. 7-8.

10. Higher Committee for Agrarian Reform, *Land Reform Law Full Text* (Cairo: Press Department, 1954), pp. 3-30.

11. Sayed Marei, *Agrarian Reform in Egypt* (Cairo: Institute of Oriental Archeology Press, 1957), p. 160.

12. *Ibid.*, p. 86.

13. *Ibid.*, p. 89.

14. Higher Committee for Agrarian Reform, *Replies to the United Nations' Questionnaires Relating to Egyptian Agrarian Reform Measures* (Cairo: Press Department, 1955), p. 40.

15. Egyptian National FAO Committee, *Report on the State of Food and Agriculture, 1953-1954* (Cairo: Les Edition Universitaires D'Egypte, 1954), p. 70.

16. Marei, p. 111.

CHAPTER IV

1. See Appendix of this study for details of methodology.

2. Higher Committee for Agrarian Reform, *Land Reform Law Full Text* (Cairo: Press Department, 1954), p. 4.

3. *Ibid.*, pp. 26-31.

4. Kenneth H. Parsons *et al.*, *Land Tenure* (Madison: University of Wisconsin Press, 1956), pp. 15-16.

5. Edmund S. Brunner *et al.*, *Farmers of the World* (New York: Columbia University Press, 1945), p. 80.

6. *Ibid.*, pp. 81-82.

7. Ministry of Social Affairs, Egypt, *Second Social Welfare Seminar for Arab States of the Middle East* (Cairo: S.O.P. Press, 1950) pp. 185-186.

8. Brunner *et al.*, pp. 1-4.

CHAPTER V

1. See Appendix of this study for details of methodology.

2. See Appendix of this study for statistical procedure, observed coefficients of correlation between the distribution patterns of the farmers in the land reform and control groups, and t values for the difference between the observed and hypothetical coefficients.

CHAPTER VI

1. Doreen Warriner, *Land Reform and Economic Development* (Cairo: National Bank of Egypt, 1955), p. 15.

2. *Ibid.*, p. 16.

3. Sayed Marei, *Agrarian Reform in Egypt* (Cairo: Institute of Oriental Archeology Press, 1957), p. vii.

4. Wilbert E. Moore, *Economic Demography of Eastern and Southern Europe* (Geneva: League of Nations, 1945), p. 100.

5. About 145,000 feddans liable to expropriation were sold privately by landowners according to Article 4 of the Agrarian Reform Law. Another 157,000 feddans were declared fallow and were not subject to immediate requisition.

6. The Higher Committee for Agrarian Reform estimated the number of new owners at 200,000 families comprised of 1.2 million individuals. This estimate was probably made on the basis of the total area liable to expropriation.

7. Warriner, p. 29.

8. Sir Malcolm Darling, "Land Reform in Italy and Egypt," *Year Book of Agricultural Cooperation, 1956* (London: Basil Blackwell, 1956).

9. Mohamed R. Ghonemy, "Resource Use and Income in Egyptian Agriculture Before and After Land Reform with Particular Reference to Economic Development," (unpublished Ph. D. dissertation, North Carolina State College, 1953), pp. 199-200.

10. Kenneth H. Parsons *et al.*, *Land Tenure* (Madison: University of Wisconsin Press, 1956), p. 598.

11. *Ibid.*, p. 602.

12. Darling.

13. Doreen Warriner, *Land Reform and Development in the Middle East* (London: Royal Institute of International Affairs, 1957), p. 43.

14. Darling
15. Warriner, pp. 6-7.
16. Frederick L. Thomsen, *Agricultural Marketing* (1st ed.; New York: McGraw-Hill, 1951), pp. 440-442.
17. National Population Commission, Egypt, *The Population Problem In Egypt* (Cairo: Permanent Council of Public Services, 1955), p. 20.
18. Moore, p. 122.
19. *Ibid.*, pp. 128-138.
20. Charles P. Issawi, *Egypt at Mid-Century, An Economic Survey* (London: Oxford University Press, 1954), p. 164.
21. *Ibid.*, p. 163.
22. *Ibid.*, p. 162.
23. Moore, pp. 140-142.
24. Warren S. Thompson, *Population Problems* (4th ed.; New York: McGraw-Hill, 1953), p. 286.
25. Alexandre Morris Carr-Saunders, *The Population Problem: A Study in Human Evolution* (Oxford: Clarendon Press, 1922), pp. 476-477.
26. Thompson, p. 198.
27. *Journal of the Egyptian Medical Association* (July, 1937). Also, *News of Population and Birth Control* (May, 1952). Also, quoted by: S. Chandrasekhar, *Population and Planned Parenthood in India* (London: George Allen and Unwin, 1955), p. 58.
28. Planning Commission, India, *The First Five Year Plan; A Draft Outline* (New Delhi: Planning Commission, 1951), pp. 206-7.
29. Interview with President Gamal Abdel Nasser by Harry Ellis and Wilton Wynn, Cairo, Egypt, October 8, 1959.

Bibliography

A. BOOKS

Abrams, Charles. *Revolution in Land*. New York: Harper and Brothers, 1939.

Ayrout, H. H. *The Fellaheen*. Cairo: R. Schindler Press, 1938.

Barclay, G. W. *Techniques of Population Analysis*. New York: John Wiley and Sons, 1958.

Barnett, H. G. *Innovation*. New York: McGraw-Hill, 1953.

Bliss, William D. P., *et al. The New Encyclopedia of Social Reforms*. Fourth edition. London: Wagnall's Company, 1908.

Boktor, Amir. *School and Society in the Valley of the Nile*. Cairo: Elias Modern Press, 1936.

Brunner, Edmund S., *et al. Farmers of the World*. New York: Columbia University Press, 1945.

Carr-Saunders, Alexandre Morris. *The Population Problem: A Study in Human Evolution*. Oxford: Clarendon Press, 1922.

Centers, Richard. *The Psychology of Social Classes*. Princeton: Princeton University Press, 1949.

Chandrasekhar, S. *Population and Planned Parenthood in India*. London: George Allen and Unwin, 1955.

Chang, P. K. *Agriculture and Industrialization*. Cambridge: Harvard University Press, 1941.

Chapin, F. Stuart. *Experimental Designs in Sociological Research*. New York: Harper and Brothers, 1947.

Clark, Colin. *The Conditions of Economic Progress*. London: Macmillan and Company, 1957.

Cleland, Wendell. *The Population Problem in Egypt*. Lancaster, Pa.: Science Press, 1936.

Cohen, R. L. *The Economics of Agriculture*. New York: Pitman Publishing Corporation, 1949.

Cromer, Evelyn Baring. *Modern Egypt*. Vol. II. London: Macmillan and Company, 1908.

Davis, Kingsley. *Human Society*. New York: The Macmillan Company, 1949.

Fairchild, H. P., *et al. Dictionary of Sociology*. Ames: Littlefield, Adams and Company, 1957.

Griswold, A. Whitney. *Farming and Democracy*. New York: Harcourt, Brace and Company, 1948.

Hagood, Margaret Jarman. *Statistics for Sociologists*. New York: Henry Holt and Company, 1941.

Hewes, Lawrence I., Jr. *Japan-Land and Men, the Story of Land Reform in Japan*. Ames: Iowa State University Press, 1955.

Infield, H. F. and J. B. Maier. *Cooperative Group Living*. New York: Koosis and Company, 1950.

Issawi, Charles P. *Egypt at Mid-Century, An Economic Survey*. London: Oxford University Press, 1954.

Jacoby, Erich H. *Agrarian Unrest in Southeast Asia*. New York: Columbia University Press, 1949.

Jesness, O. B. (ed.). *Readings on Agricultural Policy*. Philadelphia: Blakiston Company, 1949.

Laidler, Harry W. *Social-Economic Movements*. New York: Thomas Y. Crowell Company, 1949.

Lasswell, Harold D. *The World Revolution of Our Time: A Framework for Basic Policy Research*. Stanford: Stanford University Press, 1951.

Loomis, C. P. and J. A. Beegle. *Rural Social Systems*. New York: Prentice-Hall, 1950.

Mannheim, Karl. *Man and Society in an Age of Reconstruction*. New York: Harcourt, Brace and Company, 1940.

Marei, Sayed. *Agrarian Reform in Egypt*. Cairo: Institute of Oriental Archeology Press, 1957.

Marx, Karl. *The Poverty of Philosophy*. New York: International Publishers, n.d.

Merton, Robert K. *Social Theory and Social Structure*. Glencoe: Free Press, 1949.

Mills, F. C. *Statistical Methods*. 4th ed. New York: Henry Holt and Company, 1955.

Moore, W. E. *Industrialization and Labor*. Ithaca: Cornell University Press, 1951.

Mosharrafa, Maustafa M. *Cultural Survey of Modern Egypt*. London: Longmans, 1947.

Newman, Philip C. *The Development of Economic Thought*. New York: Prentice-Hall, 1952.

Ogburn, William F. *Social Change*. New York: The Viking Press, 1938.

Parsons, Kenneth H., *et al*. *Land Tenure*. Madison: University of Wisconsin Press, 1956.

Parsons, Talcott. *The Social System*. Glencoe: Free Press, 1951.

Pigou, A. C. *The Economics of Welfare*. London: Macmillan and Company, 1948.

Renne, Roland R. *Land Economics*. New York: Harper and Brothers, 1947.

Riffat, Mohamed. *The Awakening of Modern Egypt*. London: Longmans, 1947.

Roychoudhury, Makhanlal. *Egypt in 1945*. Calcutta: University of Calcutta, 1946.

Schulta, Theodore W. *The Economic Organization of Agriculture*. New York: The Macmillan Company, 1952.

Schumpeter, Joseph A. *Imperialism and Social Classes*. New York: Augustus M. Kelley, Inc., 1951.

Senior, Clarence. *Land Reform and Democracy*. Gainesville: University of Florida Press, 1958.

Sorokin, P. A. *Social and Cultural Dynamics*. Vol. III. New York: American Book Company, 1937.

Stephenson, Carl. *Medieval Feudalism*. Ithaca: Cornell University Press, 1942.

Thompson, Warren S. *Population Problems*. 4th ed. New York: McGraw-Hill, 1953.

Thomsen, Frederick L. *Agricultural Marketing*. 1st ed. New York: McGraw-Hill, 1951.

Young, George. *Egypt*. New York: C. Scribner's Sons, 1927.

B. GOVERNMENT PUBLICATIONS

Abdul-Nasser, Jamal. *Egypt's Liberation*. Washington: Public Affairs Press, 1955.

Bureau of Statistics and Census, Egypt. *Annuaire Statistique: 1951-1954*. Cairo: Government Press, 1956.

————. *Annual Statistics for Pocket: 1950-1951*. Cairo: Government Press, 1952.

————. *Population Census of Egypt, 1947*. Cairo: Government Press, 1954.

Department of Agriculture, Egypt. *Agricultural and Economic Statistics*. Cairo: Itmad Press, 1949.

————. *Monthly Agricultural Bulletin*. No. 6. October, 1949.

————. *Monthly Bulletin*. No. 7. July, 1951.

Embassy of United Arab Republic. *Egypt's New Regime*. Washington, D.C.: Press Department, 1953.

————. *Explanatory Note on Land Reform Law*. Washington, D.C.: Press Department, 1952.

————. *An Interview with President Gamal Abdel Nasser by Harry Ellis and Wilton Wynn*. Washington, D.C.: Press Department, 1959.

Gooch, Donald W. *World Land Reform*. Washington: U. S. Department of Agriculture, 1951.

Higher Committee for Agrarian Reform. *Changes in the Institutional Structure Which Form an Obstacle to Agricultural Development in Egypt*. Cairo: Press Department, 1957.

————. *Demera Estate*. Cairo: Press Department, 1953.

————. *Land Reform in Egypt*. Cairo: Press Department, 1956.

————. *Land Reform Law Full Text*. Cairo: Press Department, 1954.

————. *Land Reform Statistical Bulletin*. 2nd ed. Cairo: Statistical Department, 1956.

————. *Replies to the United Nations' Questionnaires Relating to Egyptian Agrarian Reform Measures*. Cairo: Press Department, 1955.

Ministry of Finance and National Economy, Egypt. *Public Domain Bureau, Its Establishment and Work*. Cairo: Department of Finance, 1949.

Ministry of Social Affairs, Egypt. *Second Social Welfare Seminar for Arab States of the Middle East*. Cairo: S.O.P. Press, 1950.

————. *Social Welfare in Egypt*. Cairo: S.O.P. Press, 1950.

National Population Commission, Egypt. *The Population Problem in Egypt*. Cairo: Permanent Council of Public Service, 1955.

Planning Commission. *The First Five-Year Plan; A Draft Outline*. New Delhi: Planning Commission, 1951.

Presidency of Council of Ministers, Egypt. *The Unity of the Nile Valley*. Cairo: Government Press, 1947.

Raper, Arthur F. *The Japanese Village in Transition*. Tokyo: General Headquarters, Supreme Commander for the Allied Powers, 1950.

C. PUBLICATIONS OF OTHER ORGANIZATIONS

Asiatic Regional Conference, International Labor Organization. *Economic Background of Social Policy*. New Delhi: International Labour Organization, 1947.

Badeau, Stathoff. *The Emergence of Modern Egypt*. New York: Foreign Policy Association, 1953.

Horace Plunkett Foundation. *Yearbook of Agriculture Cooperation, 1956*. London: Basil Blackwell, 1956.

International Land Tenure Research Committee. *Agricultural Land Tenure Research, Scope and Nature: Reappraisal*. Chicago: Farm Foundation, 1955.

Jacoby, Erich H. *Inter-Relationship Between Agrarian Reform and Agricultural Development*. Rome: Food and Agriculture Organization of the United Nations, 1953.

Milbank Memorial Fund. *Demographic Studies of Selected Areas of Rapid Growth*. New York: Milbank Memorial Fund, 1944.

————. *The Interrelations of Demographic, Economic, and Social Problems in Selected Under-Developed Areas*. New York: Milbank Memorial Fund, 1953.

Mitchell, C. Clyde. *Land Reform In Asia*. Washington: National Planning Association, 1952.

Moore, Wilbert E. *Economic Demography of Eastern and Southern Europe*. Geneva: League of Nations, 1945.

National Bank of Egypt. *Economic Bulletin*, Vol. VIII, No. 3. Cairo: Research Department of the Bank, 1955.

National FAO Committee, Egypt. *Report on the State of Food and Agriculture, 1953-1954*. Cairo: Les Edition Universitaires D'Egypte, 1954.

Nelson, Lowery. *Land Reform in Italy*. Washington: National Planning Association, 1956.

Poliak, A. W. *Feudalism in Egypt, Syria, Palestine and the Lebanon*. London: The Royal Asiatic Society, 1939.

United Nations. *The Consolidation of Fragmented Holdings*. Washington: Food and Agriculture Organization of the United Nations, 1950.

————. *Economic Development in the Middle East, 1945-1954*. New York: U. N. Department of Economic Affairs, 1955.

————. *Land Reform.* New York: U.N. Department of Economic Affairs, 1951.

————. *Measures for the Economic Development of Under-Developed Countries.* New York: U.N. Department of Economic Affairs, 1951.

————. *Progress in Land Reform.* New York: U.N. Department of Economic Affairs, 1954.

Warriner, Doreen. *Land Reform and Development in the Middle East.* London: Royal Institute of International Affairs, 1957.

————. *Land Reform and Economic Development.* Cairo: National Bank of Egypt, 1955.

D. UNPUBLISHED STUDIES

El-Shanawany, Haifa. "An Evaluation of the Role of the Agricultural Cooperative in the Achievement of Agrarian Reform in the Menshiah Estate." B. A. thesis, American University, Cairo, 1957.

El-Zalaky, Mohamed M.B. "An Analysis of the Organization of Egyptian Agriculture and Its Influence on Its National Economic and Social Institutions." Ph.D. dissertation, University of California, Berkeley, 1940.

Ghonemy, Mohamed Riad. "Resource Use and Income in Egyptian Agriculture Before and After Land Reform with Particular Reference to Economic Development." Ph.D. dissertation, North Carolina State College, 1953.

E. ADDRESSES

Abdul-Nasser, Jamal. Speech at El-Krion, Behira Province, Cairo, Egypt, April 19, 1956.

Brannan, Charles F. "Agriculture and National Defense." Speech before the U.S. Department of Agriculture Outlook Conference, Washington, D. C., October 30, 1950.

McCormick, Clarence J. "Beyond Today's Horizon." Opening statement before the Twelfth FAO Council Session, Rome, Italy, June 11, 1951.

Hussein, Hasan M. "Population in Relation to the Development of Agriculture." Paper presented before the World Population Conference, meeting No. 22, Rome, Italy, September, 1954.

Sparkman, John. Speech before the United Nations General Assembly, Committee Two, October 31, 1950.

F. NEWSPAPERS

New York Times, October 18, 1950.

About the Author

SAAD M. GADALLA, a native of Egypt, received his B. S. degree in Agriculture at Cairo University in 1953, served as social researcher for the Egyptian Higher Committee for Agrarian Reform, 1953-54, and was Egyptian delegate to the International Farm Youth Exchange Program in the United States in 1954. He was granted a four-year leave of absence from the Higher Committee in 1955 to study at the University of Missouri, where he received his M. S. (1956) and Ph.D. (1960) degrees in rural sociology and became assistant professor. Between 1956 and 1958, supported by the Population Council of New York, he conducted the research on the Egyptian Agrarian Reform Law which is reported in this study. Dr. Gadalla has since conducted research on farm accidents in Missouri under a three-year grant from the National Institute of Mental Health.